MW01172819

Testimonials

"Mioni's book fills a critical void in Catholic theology today, by providing a scholarly and balanced repudiation of a movement that is dividing the Catholic Church and stealing souls from the one fold of Christ: namely, a pseudo-Catholic theology that masquerades as fidelity to tradition while actually substituting private judgment, division, and insularity for authentic Catholicity. This important work will prove to be a valuable resource for both pastors and laity alike, as they grapple with the challenges wrought by traditionalism within their parishes, families, and the broader Church."

— Fr. Eric Gilbaugh
Priest of the Diocese of Helena

"Intelligent, insightful, and refreshingly charitable, *Altar Against Altar* is the book I needed but which sadly did not exist when I became a pastor in 2020. Frequently, many of the beloved sheep in my flock would express confusion about the numerous "Catholic denominations" that seem to abound. Which variety of Catholic should I be? This was a common point of anxiety and confusion. Andrew Mioni asks all the right questions in a way that cuts through the fog, avoids the red herrings, and brings new hope for anyone who wants to be a faithful and joyful Catholic in our fallen world. His book resoundingly answers several critical questions: When 'traditional Catholics' tell me that I must boycott the Novus Ordo Mass to be a good and faithful Catholic, is it true? What does authentic communion with our Holy Father and my local bishop look like? What is at the heart of the Church's authority and what does it mean to live obediently under that authority? If you desire to fearlessly live out Christ's call to be "salt and light" without rejecting the beauty of the Second Vatican Council and without breaking off communion with the Church, this book is for

i

you. I will most certainly be recommending this book to all my brother priests as well as to anyone that wants to understand how to approach 'Catholic Traditionalism' in a healthy and informed way."

— Fr Justin Hamilton
Priest of the Archdiocese of Kansas City, Kansas

"Andrew Mioni has provided the faithful with an impressive response to dissenters who undermine Christ's church under the guise of tradition. He tackles a wide range of topics, from disputes over authority to liturgical controversies, with a masterful command of the magisterium. I highly recommend all who wish to acquire the mind of the church on controversies raging in the church today to read *Altar Against Altar*."

— Michael Lofton
Host & Founder, *Reason & Theology*
Professor, Catholic Polytechnic University

"Andrew Mioni addresses the principles of Traditionalism with erudition and eloquence, and without becoming mired in the talking points of the traditionalists which obscure the fundamental issues. The phenomenon of Traditionalism has assumed an influence within wider Catholicism that I could not have foreseen as a priest of the Society of St Pius X 30 years ago. *Altar Against Altar: An Analysis of Catholic Traditionalism* is a timely and welcome answer to the pernicious movement against the Second Vatican Council. I wish it a wide audience, and trust it will assist those who struggle to accept the Council and the pontificate of Francis."

— Gary Campbell
Former SSPX priest

"Mioni's work is an indispensable guide for anyone seeking to understand the complexities of the crisis in the Catholic Church, especially as it pertains to the rise of traditionalism and the challenges posed by the Society of Saint Pius X (SSPX). The author navigates through the tumultuous waters of the Church's recent history with a keen analytical eye—as well as a remarkable breadth and depth of vision—addressing the contentious issues that arose after the Second Vatican Council. Issues caused by misinterpretation, uneven implementation, and subsequent resistance to the Council in some quarters. This is due to a faulty and ahistorical theological paradigm. Mioni's analysis of these issues is both thorough and empathetic, acknowledging the pain and confusion experienced by many in the Church, while also critiquing the self-enclosed circle mentality that often characterizes traditionalist enclaves—and he does this from a place of experience within these circles himself. In an ecclesial atmosphere where many conservatives hesitate to critique traditionalism due to a "no enemies to the right" policy, Andrew Mioni's book *Altar Against Altar* emerges as a bold and constructive contribution. It is essential reading for scholars, clergy, and laypeople who are wrestling with these issues, and offers a way forward that respects the Church's heritage while also welcoming its future."

— Andrew Likoudis
Editor, *Faith in Crisis: Critical Dialogues in Catholic Traditionalism, Church Authority, and Reform*
Associate Member, The Society for Catholic Liturgy

"*Altar Against Altar* is an important new book on the topic of 'Catholic traditionalism.' It is new in the sense that it is recent, but it is also new in the sense that it offers a perspective not yet considered, although sorely needed. This perspective entails the bracketing of all canonical specificities (debated ad nauseam and often to no avail), followed by the turning to a historical perspective, common sense, and basic principles of the Catholic faith. Instead of arguing whether this or that conciliar, liturgical, or magisterial text is the root of our woes, it asks us to consider the progressively dire trends of modernity alongside the progressively alarmed warnings of 19th and 20th century popes and theologians. Instead of arguing whether the Church canonically provides supplied jurisdiction to vagus clergy and/or priestly communities, it asks what it would mean if the Church did. Instead of arguing that there cannot be a state of necessity in the Church, it asks what it would mean if there was. *Altar Against Altar* is an important book because it brings—for the first time—a dose of common sense and a palpably Catholic spirit to an overly fraught question. It is a must-read in the midst of the polemics fueled by Denzinger-thumping armchair theologians taking place in Catholic circles on the internet."

— Dom Dalmasso
Host, *The Logos Project*
Editor-in-Chief, *The Ecclesia Blog*
M.A. Student in Dogmatic Theology, Holy Apostles College and Seminary.

"With truth and wisdom and charity, Andrew Mioni ventures into the heart of one of the great problems facing the Church today. His personal experience and detailed analysis of the various points of the traditionalist movement are simply and clearly synthesized in *Altar Against Altar*. This book is a powerful apologetic tool for those who are in traditionalist spheres, have exited from them and are trying to reorient themselves, or who have friends and relatives still under their sway; at the same time, *Altar Against Altar* provides a beautiful defense of the Catholic Church and of our need to maintain our trust in Her and remain fully united to Her and Her lawful shepherds. Andrew's work is also a humble and implicit reminder to all of us of how it is the Church's mission to save us; it's not our mission to save the Church. God promises that His Church will not fail (cfr. Mt 16:18) and He will not go back on His promise."

— Fr. Terrance J.M. Chartier, S.T.B.
Host at Mother of the Redeemer Retreat Center, Bloomington, IN

"Andrew Mioni's *Altar Against Altar* is a clear, concise, and confident response to the Traditionalist challenge to the Church. A devastating critique, it reveals that the sources of this ideological movement's internal rot are, in a strange plot twist, the same sources underlying the errors of liberalism and modernism! Andrew and I both grew up in the movement (although we never met), and from our separate personal studies of the Tradition we both came to understand a stunningly ironic fact: Traditionalism is not Traditional! His copious quotes from the Magisterium of the Church demonstrating this reality are unanswerable and irrefutable. I believe *Altar Against Altar* is a landmark contribution to this debate, and its value stems not only from the errors it refutes, but even more from the beauty of the Church's life and truth it reveals by clearing them away."

— Mr. Andrew Bartel, OP
Author, "Why I Left the Society of St. Pius X:
An Open Letter to Fr. Gołaski"

"An honest and compelling examination of Traditionalist claims, *Altar Against Altar* actually is what other books only claim to be: scholarly, easily-digestible, thought-provoking and 100% Catholic. Andrew knows his subject matter from the inside out. He charitably challenges the multiplicity of excuses that dissenting traditionalists use, and simultaneously reminds us of the beauty and wisdom inherent in the Church's structure as Christ established it. This book will long be an excellent aid for those seeking clarity for their own sake, as well as for productive dialogue with radical traditionalism. I can't recommend it too highly!"

— Laura Vander Vos
Host, *Misshappycatholic*
Creator and co-founder, TradRecovery.com

"Radical Traditionalists are rebelling against Holy Mother Church while confusing many in the process. This book does a superb job of pulling apart their claims and objections, one by one, and answering them. It is timely, well-researched, logically presented, and backed up by a plethora of sources and citations. It is an important resource that offers powerful counter arguments against Traditionalists and is very much needed in the Church today."

— Bryan Mercier
Catholic apologist, speaker, author, and President of *Catholic Truth*

"*Altar Against Altar* provides an insightful investigation into the internal contradictions of the Traditionalist worldview written in a spirit of pastoral charity with an intention to heal the rift that separates our Catholic brethren."

— Dr. Sebastian Mahfood, OP
Co-author with Ronda Chervin of *Catholic Realism*

Altar Against Altar

An Analysis of Catholic Traditionalism

Andrew Mioni

Foreword by Richard DeClue, Jr., S.Th.D.
Author of *The Mind of Benedict XVI*

En Route Books and Media, LLC
Saint Louis, MO

⚓ENROUTE
Make the time

En Route Books and Media, LLC

5705 Rhodes Avenue

St. Louis, MO 63109

Cover credit: Andrew Mioni, using with permission Ghigo Roli's photograph of "Cain and Abel sacrifice a Lamb," XII century, located in Palazzo Reale (o dei Normanni), Palermo, Sicily. Online at https://www.ghigoroli.com/. Cover texture background designed by Freepik.

ISBN-13: 979-8-88870-177-5 and 979-8-88870-205-5

Library of Congress Control Number: 2024938243

Wherefore have ye erected an altar
in opposition to the whole world?

- St. Augustine

Dedication

To my beautiful wife Clelia

Thank you for your extraordinary patience and encouragement

while I wrote this book amid a whirlwind of life circumstances.

~ ~ ~

And to Pope Benedict XVI

Thank you for opening my mind and heart with your wisdom.

I hope to meet you at the Wedding Feast one day.

Scripture passages are from the Revised Standard Version
Catholic Edition (RSV-CE)

Scripture abbreviations:

Genesis -   Gen

Exodus -   Ex

Isaiah -   Is

Jeremiah -   Jer

Matthew -   Matt

Luke -   Lk

John -   Jn

Romans -   Rom

Corinthians - Cor

Timothy -   Tim

All emphases added unless otherwise noted.

Table of Contents

Acknowledgments

I owe much gratitude to several people who helped re-shape my understanding of the Church over the last several years, and who provided the resources and assistance to make this book a reality.

To Fr. Justin Hamilton, who "showed" me the faith rather than "told" me the faith, and whose friendship and guidance has been invaluable.

To Dom Dalmasso, a former classmate who introduced me to many books and resources that I would never have considered otherwise, and for his excellent work with John Salza and Andrew Bartel in bringing clarity to this subject.

To Eric Hoyle, for his outstanding compilation of resources on the apostolicity of the Church, from which I was able to draw supporting material for several chapters.

To Andrew Likoudis, for answering my endless stream of questions about the intricacies of publishing a book, and who opened many doors for me in the process, including contributing to his volume *Faith in Crisis*.

To Fr. Eric Gilbaugh, who volunteered his time to complete a thorough proofread and offer editorial suggestions along with his testimonial.

To Dr. Richard DeClue, who took time out of his very busy schedule to provide the foreword.

To Dr. Sebastian Mahfood, OP, at En Route Books and Media, LLC, who made my lifelong dream of publishing a book come true, and who was always prompt, responsive, and available, especially with my barrage of messages asking him to make just *one* more edit.

Thank you also to all those who provided an endorsement. The fact that you considered it worth your time to read a book from a no-name individual is very humbling, and I am very grateful for your feedback.

Finally, thank you to all those who encouraged me when I was a teenager to continue my writing pursuits. I did not make my mark in the world of published literature with fantasy fiction as once I had hoped, but this is a more worthy pursuit. I hope it will provide a defense of Holy Mother Church and strengthen her unity by bringing clarity to those who are seeking answers.

Foreword

Richard G. DeClue, Jr., S.Th.D.

In recent decades, the Church has certainly faced a multifaceted crisis. Heterodoxy has been proclaimed from pulpits and in classrooms at all levels of education. Religious and clerical vocations have decreased. Cafeteria Catholicism and banal celebrations of the Most Holy Sacrifice of the Mass have become ubiquitous. This book's author, Andrew Mioni, admits this fact from the very start of Chapter 1.

Nevertheless, Mioni rightly fears that certain attempts to combat such a crisis have added fuel to the fire. As Aristotle and St. Thomas Aquinas have taught, virtue is the mean between two vices. One can fail in virtue to one extreme (privation) or to the other (excess). Along with traditionalists, Mioni recognizes the dangers of real modernism. However, he remains concerned that traditionalists sometimes fall into Satan's trap to the other extreme in ways that are—at bottom—actually self-contradictory and counterproductive. As one raised in traditionalist circles himself, he speaks from personal experience as well as from his own serious investigation into the relevant issues.

While admitting the existence of a crisis, Mioni challenges common assumptions and assertions regarding when it started, what is to blame, and what the correct response ought to be. He rebuts faulty arguments, pointing out logical and theological inconsistencies. To do so, Andrew wisely appeals to sources commonly accepted by traditionalist circles in support of his own claims and conclusions. He draws upon the Baltimore Catechism, the Council of Trent, Blessed Pius IX, Pope Benedict XV, Lateran I and IV, St. Francis de Sales, Innocent III, Pius VI, Pius X, and the 1917 Code of Canon Law.

In the process, Mioni offers a robust counter to claims coming from some traditionalist groups. The end cannot justify the means. In this vein, he appropriately pushes back against traditionalist attempts at self-justification. He calls into serious doubt the insistence on such things as extraordinary mission, state of necessity, or supplied jurisdiction. He convincingly argues that a faulty and wholly un-traditional ecclesiology is at work behind a lot of the traditionalist narratives and practices.

Notably, Andrew Mioni accomplishes all of this in a very accessible way. The book is organized thoughtfully, and the prose is very readable. The book is therefore suitable for the average reader who is interested in this important topic. Hopefully, the charitable, sincere, and honest reader who might be tempted towards a false version of traditionalism will find this book helpful for avoiding such pitfalls. Without needing to abandon legitimate concerns about the state of the Church, through this book, one can come to a more sapiential and objective assessment regarding the status of certain traditionalist sects, which—even if unintentionally—can lead people into spiritual darkness or even schism. In this day and age, it is crucial that Catholics avoid the vices associated with both liberal progressivism and radical traditionalism. This book has the potential to aid many with that task.

Introduction

What is Catholic traditionalism, or simply "traditionalism," as it is more commonly known? Why has it become such a divisive topic in recent years? What is the true purpose of its ministry?

What began as an "underground" movement decades ago has exploded into a subculture within Catholicism that has become very vocal and very influential. The last decade or so has seen the rise of many Catholic social media commentators and podcasters who are happy to lend their (sometimes quite vehement) opinions to the conversation. Few topics provoke such intense debate in Catholic circles these days as traditionalism and its various talking points, and the engagement has attracted a sizable number of followers who are discovering a new form of their faith.

But with the increase in interest, there has also come an increased exodus from the movement, especially from those who have been involved with it for the past several decades. What one demographic sees as their birthright that they were "robbed of," another sees as a jaded and bitter culture that promised to deliver spiritual fulfillment but failed to live up to that promise. So, what is the true nature of traditionalism, and should it be pursued? And most importantly, do the core tenets of traditionalism align with true Catholic tradition?

History

Catholic traditionalism refers to a phenomenon beginning after the reforms of the Second Vatican Council, which met from 1962 to

1965 to ensure the Church was prepared to meet the unprecedented challenges of the modern world. The Council reformed the Church's worship and introduced a new approach to the faith, focusing more on exhortations and the call to evangelization than on condemnations and anathemas. It intended to usher in a renewal in the life of the Catholic Church, but was immediately followed by a decrease in vocations, casual and irreverent liturgies, and poor catechesis—by all accounts, the exact opposite of what the Church had hoped to accomplish. This was due in no small part to many outside factors in the Church and society, not least of which was rampant secularism superimposed over a spiritual life in the Church that was over-reliant on externals and obligations, but for many, it was a matter of *post hoc ergo propter hoc* ("after this, therefore, because of this"). Historical and cultural context indicates that the rot of religious indifference was much stronger and had much deeper effects than what is usually indicated, as later chapters will explain, but the reforms became an easy scapegoat. It seemed clear; all these things happened immediately after the Council, and, therefore, the Council "must have been" the catalyst for them.

Seeing these "fruits" of the Council, Catholics who were dissatisfied with (or, in most cases, outright rejected) its reforms sought out priests who could provide the "traditional," pre-conciliar Mass and catechesis. Many priests, for their part, were happy to oblige, as they were just as displeased with the Church's reforms as the laity. Newsletters and networks began to establish regular schedules of Masses, whether that be in a priest's home, a church basement, or public places, leading to such things as "hotel Masses."

Several years after the close of the Council, an organization was established solely for the purpose of providing priestly formation that was based on pre-conciliar methods. This was the Society of St. Pius the Tenth, or SSPX, founded by Marcel Lefebvre, a French archbishop who was present at the Council and took issue with its most significant reforms, chief among them being the liturgy and the declaration of religious freedom in the document *Dignitatis humanae*. The SSPX was lawfully established, with the intention that its seminarians would then receive Holy Orders and subsequent assignments from their lawful bishop, but Lefebvre drew the ire of the Vatican after issuing a public statement in 1974 in which he claimed that the Council's reforms "contributed and are still contributing to the destruction of the Church, to the ruin of the priesthood, to the abolition of the Sacrifice of the Mass and of the sacraments," and that it was "therefore impossible for any conscientious and faithful Catholic to…submit to [them] in any way whatsoever."[1] This became the rallying cry of the traditionalists—that Vatican II and the Novus Ordo Missae ("New Order of Mass") were destroying the Church and must be rejected wholesale.

Naturally, this declaration caused Rome to issue a swift response. Pope Paul VI suppressed the SSPX several months later and ordered Lefebvre to cease his work. Lefebvre flatly refused, stating that the suppression was unjust and therefore null. He was subse-

---

[1] "Archbishop Lefebvre's November 21, 1974 Declaration," SSPX website. https://sspx.org/en/news-events/news/archbishop-lefebvres-november-21-1974-declaration-52771

quently suspended from public ministry in 1976 when he illicitly ordained thirteen men to the priesthood, but he ignored this penalty as well.

His public declaration added fuel to the traditionalist fire, and eventually the movement that began with individual roaming priests grew into communities and parishes established around the world, spearheaded by the SSPX. While the Church pressed on with carrying out the reforms of Vatican II, knowing that they could not be properly implemented within the span of a decade or two and simply needed more time, the traditionalists pushed back, eager to accommodate those Catholics who were clamoring for the Mass as they once knew it. It did not matter that they had not been invited by the local bishop to operate in his diocese or had not been granted the necessary faculties. The people were desperate, and their rallying cry made it quite clear; the Church and the faith itself were on the line, and no canonical impediments could deter their pursuit of preferred liturgical practices.

When John Paul II was elected in 1979, he made several attempts to bring the traditionalists back into full communion with the Church, recognizing that the Council's reforms were rather abrupt and that some may have needed more time to adjust. The first gesture was his letter *Quattuor abhinc annos* in 1984, which permitted usage of the 1962 missal under certain circumstances where the local bishop permitted it (generating the "indult Masses" from the early years of traditionalism). He also maintained dialogue with the SSPX over the next several years to find some way to reincorporate them into the Church while also upholding the teachings of the Vatican II.

His gestures were not enough, however. Limited permissions for the Mass meant little to the growing numbers of traditionalists, especially when Rome continued to promote the teachings of the Council. The SSPX threw down the gauntlet on behalf of the traditionalist movement in 1988, when Archbishop Lefebvre consecrated four bishops without the necessary papal mandate. John Paul II had agreed to grant him a bishop to continue his apostolate (an exceedingly generous act, considering Lefebvre had refused to close his seminary and cease ordaining priests as Pope Paul VI had ordered him to, and had persisted in his disobedience for almost fifteen years). Lefebvre, however, did not trust Rome, and instead of consecrating one bishop who would be chosen by the Vatican, as was agreed upon, Lefebvre proceeded to consecrate four bishops, whom he personally picked. He also performed these consecrations several months ahead of the agreed-upon date. He had made his intentions clear to the Vatican and received several warnings, but he ignored them. Episcopal consecrations conferred against the direct orders of the Pope and without the necessary mandate is a very serious offense, but the message was clear; the traditionalist cause was of such importance that it was worth defying Rome in matters of the utmost gravity.

The 1988 consecrations instigated a debate that continues to this day. Did Lefebvre and the bishops incur an excommunication for this act? The Vatican's point of view was quite clear. In his apostolic letter *Ecclesia Dei*, written to respond to this incident, Pope John Paul II said that "notwithstanding the formal *canonical warning* sent to them by the Cardinal Prefect of the Congregation for Bishops on 17 June last, Mons. Lefebvre and the priests Bernard Fellay, Bernard

Tissier de Mallerais, Richard Williamson and Alfonso de Galarreta, have incurred the grave penalty of excommunication envisaged by ecclesiastical law."[2]

Despite this declaration, the traditionalists claimed that the mitigating circumstances—namely, a grave state of necessity—removed any culpability for these actions, and that no excommunications were ever incurred. They claimed they were simply doing this to ensure that the movement would have bishops to ordain priests, who could provide the sacraments to people at a time when their spiritual formation was, to put it mildly, unpredictable. Canonical defenses were written and traditionalist "apologetics" were disseminated to reinforce the faith of leery Lefebvrists, and despite the Pope's appeal to the people of "[fulfilling] the grave duty of remaining united to the Vicar of Christ in the unity of the Catholic Church, and of ceasing their support in any way for that movement,"[3] the traditionalist movement only continued to grow.

A number of SSPX priests who heeded the Vatican's declarations were reconciled to the Church, and John Paul II permitted them to continue their ministry in its pre-conciliar form to serve the faithful who shared their hesitations of remaining affiliated with a group that was no longer in good standing with the Church. These priests formed the Priestly Fraternity of St. Peter (or FSSP, for the Latin *Fraternitas Sacerdotalis Sancti Petri*), introducing another factor into the traditionalist movement; those who were in communion

---

[2] John Paul II, *Ecclesia Dei* (1988), Vatican Archive, https://www.vatican.va/content/john-paul-ii/en/motu_proprio/documents/hf_jp-ii_motu-proprio_02071988_ecclesia-dei.html (emphasis in original)

[3] Ibid.

with the Church and offered the same Mass and sacraments, but who had, as the SSPX saw it, "compromised" their principles and succumbed to the errors of "Modernist Rome."

Since that fateful day in 1988, the movement has only continued to grow in both directions. Other canonically legitimate groups have been established, such as the Institute of Christ the King Sovereign Priest (ICKSP), while the SSPX has hemorrhaged priests and followers into countless splinter groups (including one led by their Bishop Richard Williamson after he was expelled from the Society), many of whom broke away after some dissatisfaction with SSPX leadership or ideological disagreements.

All these splinter groups, furthermore, were emboldened by the SSPX's outright rejection of any and all canonical penalties. Priests saw that a simple appeal to a "state of necessity" could exempt them from any disciplinary action, and so in their minds, they had just as much justification to break away and form their own apostolate as Lefebvre had. One group after another split off, each of them thinking they had the unsullied form of the faith that their parent organization had somehow lost, and each of them appealing to the same defenses for their ministry.

The movement continued to grow, with both licit and illicit groups establishing more chapels and communities around the world. Traditionalism primarily took root in the U.S. and France, with its American regional hubs being concentrated in the Pacific Northwest (mainly Spokane and northern Idaho), the Midwest (in Kansas City, Omaha, and others, with St Marys, KS being the SSPX's largest community), the Cincinnati area (where several different groups have established communities), and the upper east coast (New York, Connecticut, and others).

In 2007, Pope Benedict XVI extended an olive branch to them with his apostolic letter *Summorum pontificum*. Recognizing that "not a few of the faithful continued to be attached with such love and affection to the earlier liturgical forms which had deeply shaped their culture and spirit,"[4] this *motu proprio* permitted even wider usage of the 1962 missal by allowing any priest to celebrate the old form of the Mass without needing his bishop's permission. Until that time, the "Latin Mass" was only celebrated in chapels specifically established for that purpose, but Benedict XVI's declaration permitted it to be celebrated in any church. He also lifted the excommunications of the four SSPX bishops in 2009, but clarified that this was to remove the ecclesiastical impediment to reconciliation, and that "until the doctrinal questions are clarified, the Society has no canonical status in the Church, and its ministers – even though they have been freed of the ecclesiastical penalty – do not legitimately exercise any ministry in the Church."[5]

The traditionalist movement continued to gain more followers as the faithful sought out reverent liturgies, earning a particular

---

[4] Benedict XVI, *Summorum pontificum* (2007) Vatican Archive, https://www.vatican.va/content/benedict-xvi/en/motu_proprio/documents/hf_ben-xvi_motu-proprio_20070707_summorum-pontificum.html

[5] Benedict XVI, "Letter of His Holiness Pope Benedict XVI to the bishops of the Catholic Church concerning the remission of the excommunication of the four bishops consecrated by Archbishop Lefebvre," Vatican Archive, https://www.vatican.va/content/benedict-xvi/en/letters/2009/documents/hf_ben-xvi_let_20090310_remissione-scomunica.html

boost in the 2010s thanks to social media and online personalities. Those who sought out the "Latin Mass" often knew little to nothing about which group of priests offered it or whether they were in good standing with the Church. The reverence and the splendor was worth it to them after being subjected to casual, irreverent, or otherwise unsatisfactory liturgies over the years.

In 2015, several years after being elected to the papacy, Pope Francis declared that SSPX priests could validly and licitly absolve sins in the sacrament of Penance. He then extended this faculty indefinitely after the Jubilee Year of Mercy that began in 2015. In 2017, he also urged diocesan bishops to grant SSPX priests the faculty to witness marriages (a priest must have jurisdiction to validly absolve sins and witness marriages). The SSPX thanked Pope Francis for the gesture but maintained that their priests always had supplied jurisdiction to administer the sacraments (which will be discussed in Chapter 6), and regarded this as little more than a formality. (These concessions were not granted to any other independent groups, of which there were quite a few by the 2010s. Further details can be found in Chapter 11.)

In 2021, the traditionalist movement again became the subject of the Vatican's attention when Pope Francis issued his apostolic letter *Traditionis custodes*, in which he abrogated *Summorum pontificum* and once again placed permissions for usage of the 1962 missal in the hands of the bishops, as John Paul II had done. He cited increasing divisions in the Church, stating in its accompanying letter that the permissions granted by John Paul II and Benedict XVI were "exploited to widen the gaps, reinforce the divergences, and encourage disagreements that injure the Church, block her path, and expose her to the peril of division."[6] Since then, the traditionalist movement has become a greater point of controversy, with many becoming more vehement in their assertions that the "Latin Mass" is the future of the Church, as was evident by the "persecution" against it from "Modernist Rome."

It is with honesty and with understanding that we should examine the motivations of the traditionalists. Any Catholic who grew up during the 1970s and 1980s can attest to a stark difference between their experience at Sunday Mass and their parents' experience several decades prior. Nobody can deny that the years immediately following Vatican II were a mess, and the Church is still navigating her way through the fallout of an abysmal initial implementation of the reforms. But traditionalism is not the answer, and the objective of this book is to explain why.

Traditionalism

For the purposes of this book, I understand traditionalism as an "-ism," as an ideology distinct from what some might call "traditional Catholicism." I personally find it redundant to add a qualifier in this context. To be Catholic means to be traditional, and to describe oneself using this prefix implies that there is also such a thing

---

[6] Francis, "Letter of the Holy Father Francis to the bishops of the whole world, that accompanies the Apostolic Letter motu proprio data *Traditionis custodes*," July 16, 2021, Vatican Archive, https://www.vatican.va/content/francesco/en/letters/2021/documents/20210716-lettera-vescovi-liturgia.html

as non-traditional Catholicism. As Pope Benedict XV wrote, "Catholics should abstain from certain appellations which have recently been brought into use to distinguish one group of Catholics from another. [...] There is no need of adding any qualifying terms to the profession of Catholicism: it is quite enough for each one to proclaim 'Christian is my name and Catholic my surname,' only let him endeavour to be in reality what he calls himself."[7] Preferring older devotions or older forms of the liturgy does not set us apart from our Catholic neighbors as "more traditional," and as such, I do not regard legitimately established groups like the FSSP as "traditionalists." The ideology may be present in their congregations, but they do operate within the juridical structure of the Church and do possess delegated jurisdiction for their ministry. They should be regarded simply as "Catholics," no more, no less.

To call oneself a "traditionalist," however, is entirely different. Traditionalism is its own unique entity, characterized by juridical separation from the governing structure of the Church and by its self-willed independence from lawful diocesan authority. It also operates in a stagnated existence in which everything the Church has proclaimed since Vatican II is suspect, even with full magisterial weight behind certain declarations. The traditionalist position rests on previous magisterial teachings and previous catechisms, essentially bringing the Church to a standstill with no indication as to when it will resume its governance with "untainted" teachings. As Yale scholar Jaroslav Pelikan said, "Tradition lives in conversation

---

[7] Benedict XV, *Ad beatissimi apostolorum* (1914), Vatican Archive, https://www.vatican.va/content/benedict-xv/en/encyclicals/documents/hf_ben-xv_enc_01111914_ad-beatissimi-apostolorum.html

with the past, while remembering where we are and when we are and that it is we who have to decide. Traditionalism supposes that nothing should ever be done for the first time, so all that is needed to solve any problem is to arrive at the supposedly unanimous testimony of this homogenized tradition."[8] An accurate representation of the Catholic traditionalist movement if ever there was one.

There are two main schools of thought in traditionalism. The first is the "Recognize and Resist" faction, primarily led by the SSPX, which, as the name indicates, recognizes that the Second Vatican Council, the pope and bishops, and the new forms of the Mass and sacraments are, strictly speaking, valid and legitimate, but it nonetheless believes that they have introduced confusion, error, and even heresy into the Church, and therefore must be rejected. (Contradictions abound when comparing their official position to their actions, however; they publicly state that the new forms of the sacraments are valid but, based on erroneous understandings of sacramental intention perpetrated by their founder, their priests regularly recommend or administer conditional sacraments "just in case." The belief that the new forms of the sacraments are of dubious validity is a very common one among Recognize and Resist adherents.)

The second faction is the sedevacantists (from the Latin *sede vacante*, or "empty seat"), represented by groups like the Congregation of Mary Immaculate Queen (CMRI, for the Latin *Congregatio Mariae Reginae Immaculatae*) led by Mark Pivarunas. Sedevacantists believe that every pope since Pius XII has been a heretic

---

[8] Joseph Carey, "Christianity as an Enfolding Circle [Conversation with Jaroslav Pelikan]" (June 26, 1989), U.S. News & World Report. Vol. 106, no. 25. p. 57.

and antipope, and therefore never held the position of the papacy at all. They believe there is currently no pope, the bishops of the world hold no authority, the new form of the Mass and sacraments are invalid, and that the "true faith" lies in their communities that exclusively celebrate the old forms of the Mass and sacraments.

There are also several other fringe groups. Sedeprivationists believe that the sitting pope holds the material but not formal office of the papacy. Former "Benevacantists" believe that Pope Benedict XVI's resignation was invalid, as it was done under duress, and that he was the last legitimate pope (naturally, they have become sedevacantists by default after his passing). There are also any number of independent chapels led by single priests who departed from both factions and whose beliefs are unknown, but these are the minority even within the traditionalist minority.

Ideologies bleed between the two groups, with sedevacantists lurking in the ranks of their Recognize and Resist brethren. Individuals in licit groups like the FSSP often also hold to the Recognize and Resist mindset and would not hesitate to attend an SSPX chapel if their church were to be suppressed by the local bishop.

All traditionalists operate under the same standards. Their bishops are consecrated without the necessary mandate from the Holy See and have not been granted jurisdiction over any priest or any diocese by the Holy See. Their priests are ordained without the dimissorial letters required by canon law, by bishops who are not their lawful superiors. Their priests carry out a public ministry worldwide, without being incardinated (i.e., legally delegated) into any diocese or being authorized to do so by any lawful bishop. These are facts that even they will not deny.

Despite all these irregularities, the traditionalists claim that their work is not only justified, but necessary. Their rationale is that a full-scale ministry operating separately from the established order is required to combat the "errors" of Vatican II and to maintain "true tradition" in the Church. Citing canon 1752, which states that "the salvation of souls…must always be the supreme law in the Church,"[9] traditionalist clergy claim that they are simply providing the sacraments to the faithful to foster the salvation of souls, and that a grave "state of necessity" allows them to circumvent the usual ecclesiastical and canonical boundaries to do so.

These are bold claims, and the salvation of souls does indeed hang in the balance. Should the faithful turn to those who are willing to provide sacraments and catechesis in a manner that appears more traditional and reverent, or should they remain in union with their bishop and their diocese despite potential hardships?

Personal History

I approach this topic after a long personal history with the traditionalist movement. Both of my parents were raised in the SSPX, and both sides of my (very large) family still attend their chapels. My parents made the decision not to raise us in the SSPX, but I grew up attending an FSSP chapel in Maple Hill, Kansas, in the shadow of the SSPX's epicenter of St. Mary's, only ten minutes away. Though

---

[9] 1983 Code of Canon Law, c. 1752, in *Code of Canon Law*, Vatican Archive, https://www.vatican.va/archive/cod-iuris-canonici/eng/documents/cic_lib7-cann1732-1752_en.html#SECTION_II

we were connected to the diocese, I still grew up under the impression that the Novus Ordo Missae was deficient, that Vatican II was not necessary, and that the Church really ought to return to the "traditional" ways to move forward. I attended St. Mary's Academy for several years of high school, during which I was suddenly subjected to such narratives from their priests as Freemasons infiltrating the Vatican and maneuvering Vatican II, a "Protestant Mass" imposed by the Pope, and why the FSSP parish that I and my family attended was "compromised" and why I really should not be attending there. So, I had many questions; questions which uncovered my family's long history with the traditionalist movement, of which, until then, I was more or less unaware. I also lived in St Marys for a time during college and regularly interacted with the SSPX adherents there.

I met the woman who would become my wife at St. Mary's Academy. Born and raised in the SSPX, she had been taught the traditionalist narrative from the time she was very young, but by the grace of God, she was open to hearing me out when I told her I was not at all comfortable raising my family in the SSPX. How could I expect my children to recognize my paternal authority if I and the community in which I was raising them did not acknowledge the authority of any Church officials and operated by their own standards? A former SSPX priest, Abbé Emmanuel Berger, had put words to my dilemma in 1994: "Through constantly criticizing authority at its different levels, schools, State, priests, bishops, Pope, do we not end by destroying in the heart of the faithful, and especially of the children, the very principle of authority?"[10] I simply could not do that. This prompted extensive research into the traditionalist narrative so that we could be on the same spiritual page, and we plumbed the depths of the traditionalists' resources, their defenses, and the teachings of the Church to make an informed decision on the matter.

What we discovered shattered the foundations of my wife's upbringing and put the traditionalist movement in an entirely new light for both of us, especially after reading the writings of Pope Benedict XVI. Unbeknownst to us, we were doing exactly what Vatican II had urged the faithful to do—reading Scripture and growing in our knowledge of it, establishing our faith on the teachings of the Church fathers, and moderating our over-reliance on things like private revelation and personal devotions. We came to understand the admirable motivations behind reforming the liturgy, which until then we had mistakenly understood as the machinations of some radicalized prelates. We also grew in our understanding of the Eucharist, communion in the Church, and the importance of maintaining unity and oneness that is indispensable for the Body of Christ. St. John Henry Newman once said, "To be deep in history is to cease to be Protestant." After several years of research and prayer, my wife quipped, "To be deep in history is to cease to be traditionalist."

---

[10] Abbé Emmanuel Berger to Bishop Bernard Fellay, June 30, 1994, *Why Do Priests Leave the SSPX?* https://www.tapatalk.com/groups/ignis_ardens/viewtopic.php?f=11&t=11560&sid=7bde664ef4a544b05fb9a-1924a9c57db&view=print.

In early 2023, I had the privilege of assisting Laura Vander Vos with establishing Trad Recovery, a support group that provided resources and community to those who were exiting the traditionalist sphere and coming into full communion with the Church. After Pope Francis' motu proprio *Traditionis Custodes* restricted the celebration of the so-called "Latin Mass," the movement attracted more followers who wanted to find out the source of the subsequent outrage and who were entranced by this liturgy they had never experienced, but it also began to alienate those who were becoming more and more dissatisfied with the movement.

The response to Trad Recovery has been overwhelmingly positive, with former traditionalists expressing their gratitude that something so necessary was finally established. Traditionalists tend to paint a grim picture of the Church today, often appealing to anecdotal evidence from the years immediately following Vatican II and leading many to believe they will lose their faith entirely if they leave the traditionalist haven. But I, my wife, and many others we knew had experienced only positive things at our local diocesan church, and the traditionalist warnings were appearing weaker as we continued to investigate. The frustrations of those who recently discovered the Latin Mass were being shouted through a virtual megaphone in the Catholic world, but those who joined Trad Recovery expressed a similar outrage, frustrated that what they had been told about the Church for so long was simply untrue. Clown masses were not rampant, the Eucharist was not being carelessly scattered across the floor, and congregations were not lacking children. What their grandparents and parents experienced decades ago was not what they were seeing, and there was finally a central place to connect and share thoughts, experiences, advice, and resources for learning their way out.

My intention with this book is to help put to words the ideas and principles that changed our minds. I have found that deliberating over canonical minutiae or sparring with quotes from prelates who have voiced their opinions on the matter is not a productive strategy. Debates on traditionalism tend to rely too heavily on the "argument from authority" fallacy, i.e., citing a defense based on someone's credentials and status instead of the substance of the argument itself (which St. Thomas Aquinas described as the weakest form of argument). Bishops, priests, and canon lawyers will all disagree. Clearly, the matter will not be settled this way. But there is objective truth, and I found it to be in Catholic history and tradition as I engaged some very practical and logical questions that nobody could answer.

I will not be attempting to answer the typical questions about whether their masses fulfill the Sunday obligation, whether the excommunications were valid, and so on. These questions are often posed with the intention of simply easing one's conscience to feel justified in attending a traditionalist community, not with the intention of understanding the full picture of traditionalism as it relates to the Church. This book intends to explore the fundamentals of the movement. I will primarily present material from the SSPX, but only because they are the "face" of the movement and have published the most comprehensive content about the traditionalist ministry. I intend to respond to the movement as a whole, not to any particular group within it.

What I hope to demonstrate here is that, while indeed there is a crisis in the Church today and likely will be for some time, this crisis was not caused by nor is perpetuated by the teachings of the Second Vatican Council and the missal of Pope St. Paul VI. The crisis has generated from massive cultural and societal upheavals since the late 19th century, and, as such, establishing a worldwide independent ministry to combat it is a mistake. I hope to show that the traditionalist response is not the solution to the crisis in the Church, and that the central tenets of Catholic traditionalism do not hold up to scrutiny. For all those who are investigating the traditionalist movement, for those who have left it and are looking for more information, or for anyone who might want to discover more about this phenomenon, I hope and pray that this book is helpful.

PART I

A HISTORICAL OVERVIEW

1.

A Crisis of Authority

At the root of the traditionalist movement is the question of the crisis in the Church. It must be said from the outset—a crisis most certainly exists. Vocations have declined in the West, catechesis is lacking, and there is a profound lack of faith in our present day. To deny this would be to ignore reality. I do not at all intend to downplay the severity of the current situation in the Church and the world. But the *cause* of the crisis must be identified if we are to determine how the Church can overcome it, and this is where the traditionalist position falls short. It would demonstrate a very shortsighted view of history and culture to think that the foundations for it had not already been laid in the decades leading up to Vatican II, or that it can be mended by simply adhering to the liturgical rites and catechisms which were in use when the crisis was festering in society and which did not hold it at bay.

According to the traditionalist narrative, Modernism is to blame. They claim that Vatican II was guided by Modernism and deliberately ushered error into the Church, which then influenced the liturgical reform and laid the groundwork for a massive implosion of faith. Led by the SSPX, which took its name from the great foe of Modernism, Pope St. Pius X, traditionalists believe that the Church will be restored to its former glory once all vestiges of this perceived Modernism are cleansed. This naturally would mean that Vatican II must be redacted, the new missal must be abrogated, and the Church must return to its former state as it was circa 1960.

But the crisis runs much deeper than that, and it would be unrealistic to think that it would simply vanish if the Church reversed course. Pope Benedict XVI recognized that this crisis is of vast cultural and historical scope when he wrote, "The crisis concerning the Church, as it is reflected in the crisis concerning the concept 'People of God', is a 'crisis about God': it is the result of leaving out what is most essential."[1] This is a crisis that envelopes the moral fabric of society as it has developed for the last several hundred years. Its roots are in a dual source: the increasingly rationalistic and materialistic state of the world as it has been developing since the Middle Ages, and the state of spiritual formation during this same period, which has placed the faith within legalistic boundaries and divorced it from the pursuit of virtue.

Modernism is indeed one of its sources, as the traditionalists hold. But the term "Modernism" is often wielded in broad terms, without a thorough understanding of what it entails. The traditionalists have associated it with anything post-Vatican II for so long that its true meaning has been obscured. Pope St. Pius X wrote in his encyclical *Pascendi dominici gregis:*

> Modernists place the foundation of religious philosophy in
> that doctrine which is usually called Agnosticism. According
> to this teaching human reason is confined entirely within the
> field of phenomena, that is to say, to things that are percep-

---

[1] Joseph Ratzinger, *Pilgrim Fellowship of Faith: The Church as Communion*, trans. Henry Taylor (San Francisco; Ignatius Press, 2005), 129.

tible to the senses, and in the manner in which they are per-
ceptible; it has no right and no power to transgress these limits. Hence it is incapable of lifting itself up to God, and of
recognising His existence, even by means of visible things.[2]

Modernism, at its root, is guided by the same materialistic principles as the modern intellectual shifts of the last several centuries.
The modern age has led humanity to believe it can construct a future
based on its own discoveries, leading to a rejection of divine authority. This means that God is reduced to opinion, and His authority
cannot be invoked to guide the moral formation of the world. Benedict XVI wrote in his book *Christianity and the Crisis of Cultures*
that "the poverty of our age [is] that we now think and live only in
terms of function" and that our culture is based on "a purely functional rationality that has shaken the moral consciousness in a way
completely unknown to the cultures that existed previously, since it
maintains that only that which can be demonstrated experimentally
is 'rational.'" By this standard, the existence of God "may be denied
altogether or considered unprovable and uncertain and, hence, as
something belonging to the sphere of subjective choices. In either
case, God is irrelevant to public life."[3]

An existence based on "purely functional rationality" strips the
spiritual realities from our physical world and reduces everything to

---

[2] Pius X, *Pascendi dominici gregis* (1907), Vatican Archive,
https://www.vatican.va/content/pius-x/en/encyclicals/documents/hf_p-
x_enc_19070908_pascendi-dominici-gregis.html

[3] Joseph Ratzinger, *Christianity and the Crisis of Cultures*, trans. Brian
McNeil (San Francisco; Ignatius Press, 2006), 20 (Kindle edition).

its usefulness. If it cannot be harnessed, quantified, or utilized for a specific cause, it is meaningless. There is no longer any such thing as objective truth because truth belongs to the moral sphere and cannot be measured. Religion therefore becomes a personal choice, not a guiding force for the growth of civilization.

The development of this functional mentality reaches back centuries, sprouting from a world that had become increasingly man-centered since the Middle Ages. The seeds of the crisis were sown in the aftermath of the Protestant Reformation, which severed the singular authority from Christianity and left religious questions in the hands of individuals. As Hans Urs von Balthasar wrote, this paved the way for the Enlightenment when "people sought a position that could neutralize the opposition of denominations by attempting to reduce them to the level of criteria that can stand their ground before human reason."[4] These ideological seeds then grew in the rationalistic soil of the Enlightenment and sprouted in the materialism of the Industrial Revolution, movements that reshaped the face of the earth and challenged the long-held views of faith and religion by offering to humanity a bountiful reward of its own efforts. This was followed by a time in which communism, nihilism, and other destructive ideologies were taking hold, promising fulfillment that they claimed religion could not bring. A highly materialistic world in an atheistic culture would bring nothing but disaster to the Church.

It is a mistake to think that the Church was unaffected by these errors before Pope Pius X sounded the alarm bells on Modernism.

---

[4] Hans Urs von Balthasar, *A Short Primer for Unsettled Laymen*, trans. Michael Waldstein (San Francisco; Ignatius Press, 1985), 42.

His predecessors similarly identified these issues in no uncertain terms. As early as 1835, Pope Gregory XVI lamented the state of the world in his encyclical *Mirari vos* with the following words: "The divine authority of the Church is opposed and her rights shorn off. She is subjected to human reason and with the greatest injustice exposed to the hatred of the people and reduced to vile servitude."[5] Several decades later in 1863, Bl. Pope Pius IX echoed these sentiments in his encyclical *Quanto conficiamur moerore*: "Never will there be grief enough over the corruption of morals so extensively increasing and promoted by…the deadly virus of unbelief and indifferentism spread far and wide; by contempt for ecclesiastical authority, …by the diabolical hatred of Christ, his Church, teaching, and of this Apostolic See."[6] Pope Leo XIII wrote in his 1902 encyclical *Fin dal principio*, "It is seen everywhere how the spirit of naturalism tends to penetrate every part of the social body, even the most healthy; a spirit which fills the minds with pride and causes them to rebel against every authority; depraves the heart and turns it after the desire of earthly goods, neglecting those eternal."[7]

Even before his thunderous denunciation of Modernism, Pope Pius X issued a warning to the world in his 1903 encyclical *E supremi*

---

[5] Gregory XVI, *Mirari vos* (1832), Papal Encyclicals Online, https://www.papalencyclicals.net/greg16/g16mirar.htm

[6] Pius IX, *Quanto conficiamur moerore* (1863), Papal Encyclicals Online, https://www.papalencyclicals.net/pius09/p9quanto.htm

[7] Leo XIII, *Fin dal principio* (1902), Vatican Archive, https://www.vatican.va/content/leo-xiii/en/encyclicals/documents/hf_l-xiii_enc_0812-1902_fin-dal-principio.html

that quite clearly identified a dire situation facing the Church long before Vatican II was convened.

> For who can fail to see that society is at the present time, more than in any past age, suffering from a terrible and deep-rooted malady which, developing every day and eating into its inmost being, is dragging it to destruction? You understand, Venerable Brethren, what this disease is —apostasy from God, than which in truth nothing is more allied with ruin, according to the word of the Prophet: "For behold they that go far from Thee shall perish" (Ps. lxxii., 17). [...] [M]an has with infinite temerity put himself in the place of God, raising himself above all that is called God; in such wise that although he cannot utterly extinguish in himself all knowledge of God, he has contemned God's majesty and, as it were, made of the universe a temple wherein he himself is to be adored. "He sitteth in the temple of God, showing himself as if he were God" (II. Thess. ii., 2).[8]

These warnings from the Church should give us pause about casting blame at a council or a new missal. The world had been sinking into a self-absorbed stupor for over a hundred years before the reforms of the twentieth century. Should we really be so shocked that the practice of faith and of intellectual assent to truth has declined when a tidal wave of secularism has decimated our culture?

---

[8] Pius X, *E supremi* (1903), Vatican Archive, https://www.vatican.va/content/pius-x/en/encyclicals/documents/hf_p-x_enc_04101903_e-supremi.html

Can we blame the Church for all our woes, when things like prom-iscuity, the pursuit of wealth, and an utter lack of charity for our neighbor are practiced, advertised, and encouraged to the extent that they have been for the last hundred years or so? The decades preceding the Council were not enveloped in the spiritual triumph that some might think.

The historian Christopher Dawson wrote that the primary threat to modern culture is not a "rational hostility of a determined minor-ity, but the existence of a great mass of opinion which is not anti-religious but sub-religious, so that it is no longer conscious of any spiritual need for Christianity to fulfill."[9] The vitality of the Church is likewise threatened by a world that does not have any use for it among the conglomeration of industries and material distractions that can yield objective gratification. Religion has become little more than sentimental feeling, and since it does not impact one's liveli-hood or serve any tangible purpose, it can simply be discarded.

Despite the historical circumstances, traditionalists are quick to point out that the statistics of Catholic adherents, religious voca-tions, and Mass attendance sharply declined in the years following the Second Vatican Council. This is certainly true. But again, there are external factors that account for this in a much more plausible way than potentially malicious intentions on the part of scheming clergy. The answer was given by Pope Pius XI in 1937 when he wrote the following in his encyclical *Divini redemptoris*:

---

[9] Christopher Dawson, *The Crisis of Western Education* (New York; Sheed and Ward, 1961), 172.

Even in Catholic countries there are still too many who are Catholics hardly more than in name. There are too many who fulfill more or less faithfully the more essential obligations of the religion they boast of professing, but have no desire of knowing it better, of deepening their inward conviction, and still less of bringing into conformity with the external gloss the inner splendor of a right and unsullied conscience, that recognizes and performs all its duties under the eye of God. We know how much Our Divine Savior detested this empty pharisaic show, He Who wished that all should adore the Father "in spirit and in truth." The Catholic who does not live really and sincerely according to the Faith he professes will not long be master of himself in these days when the winds of strife and persecution blow so fiercely, but will be swept away defenseless in this new deluge which threatens the world. And thus, while he is preparing his own ruin, he is exposing to ridicule the very name of Christian.[10]

This "new deluge" that Pius XI referenced is "the atheistic movements existing among the masses of the Machine Age [that] had their origin in that school of philosophy which for centuries had sought to divorce science from the life of the Faith and of the Church."[11] This is the exact threat to the Church and the world that had been identified by many of his predecessors, and one that Pius

---

[10]   Pius XI, *Divini redemptoris* (1937), Vatican Archive, https://www.vatican.va/content/pius-xi/en/encyclicals/documents/hf_p-xi_enc_19370319_divini-redemptoris.html

[11] Ibid.

XI knew would overpower a practice of the faith that was simply routine motions or a list of memorized facts.

Pius XI identified what Fr. Servais Pinckaers would later describe as the "morality of obligation," which had dominated Catholic moral theology since the Middle Ages and was admittedly deficient in spiritual formation. In his book *Morality: The Catholic View*, Pinckaers explains that from the earliest centuries until the Middle Ages, moral theology was primarily directed toward the pursuit of happiness and the conformity of one's life to the person of Jesus Christ, guided by the Scriptures and the writings of the Church Fathers. The moral life was centered on understanding and living out the virtues, as can clearly be seen in the *Summa*. The virtues, the gifts of the Holy Spirit, and the Beatitudes were given pride of place in spiritual formation.

This would be upended in the 14th century with the introduction of nominalism, which reoriented moral theology to the domain of obligation and reduced it to laws, human acts, conscience, and sins. Theology was pared down to legal imperatives to more effectively convey the moral law in instructional manuals, which became prominent in the 17th century for priests to use in catechesis. As Pinckaers wrote of this period, "The moral law expresses the divine will, which is perfectly free and sovereign, while it limits human freedom by commanding or forbidding certain actions with the force of obligation. Law is the source of morality."[12] This created a divorce

---

[12] Servais Pinckaers, *Morality: The Catholic View*, trans. Michael Sherwin, O.P. (South Bend; St. Augustine's Press, 2001), 72.

between morality and happiness, which "altered the most fundamental notion in moral theology: the conception of the good. [...]
[D]efined by its conformity to legal obligation, the good is understood as separated from happiness and even as opposed to it."[13]

Thus, for hundreds of years, "[o]bedience to law encroached on
charity and the virtues," and "the social and ecclesial dimensions of
the Christian life were neglected."[14] Morality became less about pur-
suing happiness through virtue, giving way to a strict, legalistic form
of faith. The Church anchored its teachings in proclamations of
"thou shalt not," which, as Pinckaers explains, do have their place,
but when moral teaching does not advance beyond this and does not
show how obligations are meant to "teach the rudiments, the essential precepts, and to delineate those things without which virtue is
not possible,"[15] the faith is disconnected from personal happiness
and fulfillment. And in a time when the world offers immediate gratification in material things, those who understand their faith as a set
of externals or a list of obligations to fulfill will not be convicted by
it, because it has become a projection of faith which is not truly mo-
tivated by virtue. Happiness will be sought in pleasures of the world
rather than in true formation of the mind and heart toward God. As
Pope Benedict XVI wrote, "The law became a burden the moment it
was no longer being lived out from within but was broken down into
a series of obligations external in their origin and their nature. Thus

---

[13] Ibid, 75.
[14] Ibid, 40.
[15] Ibid, 110.

the Lord tells us emphatically: The true law of God is not an external matter. It dwells within us."[16]

Understanding these two massively influential factors, it should be obvious that the Church and her worship are not responsible for the decline in religious practice following the Council. Abuses and the failure to correct them certainly did not help, but we must also consider the societal changes that were occurring around this time. The 20th century radically reshaped the face of the world with its unprecedented advancements in technology, the insatiable desire for material wealth, and the power by which entire nations could be subdued. Two world wars generated a craving for power and an absolute disdain for human life. Scientific and technological advancements that permitted instant communication, faster travel, and constant entertainment were suddenly available to all. Humanity succumbed to the same temptation as Adam and Eve as we became convinced that we did not need God and could be gods ourselves, attempting to construct our own Garden of Eden here on earth and completely rejecting divine sovereignty.

Looking through the catechisms and the instructional material used during this period (material that is still used by traditionalists today, as they reject the current catechism), one finds a very consistent pattern that verifies the deficiencies identified by Pinckaers, which may give some indication of the unsteady foundations of Catholicism at the time. They were foundations that were crumbling, disguised under a veneer of formalities and impressive rubrics. I and many others who were raised in traditionalist environments have

---

[16] Joseph Ratzinger, *God Is Near Us: The Eucharist, the Heart of Life*, trans. Henry Taylor (San Francisco; Ignatius Press, 2003), 105.

experienced this firsthand, and we can attest that our faith resembled a checklist more than a way of life. One is reminded of the Lord's words: "[T]his people...honor me with their lips, while their hearts are far from me, and their fear of me is a commandment of men learned by rote[.]" (Is 29:13)

The years preceding the Council were primed for a decline in religious adherence. The faith was primarily presented as a set of obligations and a list of repercussions for violating those obligations, formed by memorization and habit. As C.S. Lewis so accurately wrote in the early 1950s, "People often think of Christian morality as a kind of bargain in which God says, 'If you keep a lot of rules I'll reward you, and if you don't I'll do the other thing.'"[17] This form of the faith could not withstand the lures of materialistic contentment, especially during the latter half of the 20th century which was characterized by unprecedented consumerism, entertainment in the form of media in every household, and the dawning digital age, not to mention the sexual revolution, social movements that rejected all forms of authority, and other challenges. "The other thing" Lewis mentions that awaited those who did not "follow the rules" was no longer a sufficient motivator, and the "reward" certainly was not any more so. Why struggle through life chasing spiritual happiness in theological abstractions when unlimited material happiness could be had here and now?

Are we to believe that the distractions of the modern world would hold no sway over the faithful as long as they adhered to a more externally "traditional" mode of the faith? Without delving

---

[17] C.S. Lewis, *Mere Christianity* (1952; New York, HarperCollins, 2001), 92.

into too much cynicism, my experience has shown that many in traditionalist circles succumb just as easily to these worldly attractions and do indeed view the Mass and sacraments simply as obligations to fulfill, having no interest in deepening their knowledge of biblical history or studying the patristic sources of the faith. Low attendance at Mass, unbelief in the Real Presence, poor catechesis, and all the things the Church struggles with today would still be present even if no reforms had ever taken place. Supporters of the "crisis" theory place too much stock in the supposed deficiency of a certain missal or the alleged ambiguities of a council's declarations and fail to consider that the cause of the crisis might in fact be our weak and fallen human nature, which has not had adequate spiritual formation in the manualist, rules-based format that the Church had followed for so long.

The source of the crisis certainly cannot be narrowed down to one specific factor. It has erupted from a combination of many different elements which all intertwine and create a quagmire of godlessness that rears its head in a challenge to supernatural faith. Christopher Dawson described a survey that was taken in 1951, in which respondents admit that their lack of spirituality is for quite simple and practical reasons. One says religion is "kids' stuff," another says it is useless if it cannot pay the bills, another thinks it is a matter of personal taste, and so on.[18] Dawson concluded that the results of this survey show that "the real cause of modern irreligion is not intellectual," but is based in "sheer indifference," and displays a "practical

---

[18] Dawson, 171-172.

paganism" of people who "cannot see that Christianity has any relevance to their actual lives."[19] It was a faith that no longer served any purpose and yielded no measurable results, and as the functional mindset of the 20th century dictated, it must therefore be abandoned.

As stated, a crisis most certainly exists. But it is too simple to think that it is rooted in a single, objective source that can be uprooted by practicing the faith in a manner that the Church determined was insufficient for meeting the challenges of the modern age. Even the SSPX, when pressed, is honest enough to admit that the causes are rooted in philosophy, theology, morality, and politics.[20] How will centuries of philosophy, theology, morality, and politics be overcome? We must have the honesty to admit that the scope of this crisis far exceeds the traditionalists' diagnosis of it as we proceed with examining their stance on the Council.

---

[19] Ibid, 171.

[20] "The crisis: problems, causes, remedies," SSPX website. https://sspx.org/en/crisis-problems-causes-remedies

2.

The Second Vatican Council

Vatican II was a landmark event for the Catholic Church. It was the largest gathering of bishops the world had ever seen, truly representing the Catholicity, or universality, of the Church. It was called by Pope John XXIII, who was considered by many to be a "transitional" pope, someone who was not expected to take any drastic steps while in office. It was also held during a time when mass media was becoming very prominent, and the Church took a huge risk in allowing an event of such magnitude to be covered by a secular force that would inevitably twist the proceedings to fit its own agenda. Despite these unique factors, the Church considers the Council to be one of the most important events in its history, issuing its teachings in a series of theological discourses to help renew the life of the Church and urging all to follow the universal call to holiness.

However, the traditionalists paint a different picture of the Council. They protest that councils have only been called to address whatever heresy was threatening the Church, and that Vatican II did not address any specific heresy or error. They claim that since it did not issue any anathemas or dogmatic pronouncements, and merely dealt with disciplinary matters, its declarations are not strictly binding on the faithful. The most serious of their accusations is that the Council did in fact promulgate positive error (i.e., contradictions to its previous declarations, and a rite of Mass that was deficient and spiritually harmful), and the faithful therefore have an obligation to reject it if they are to remain faithful to "Tradition." The traditionalists indeed believe that Vatican II is the culprit in the current crisis scenario and that the crisis will not be abated until the Council is redacted.

The first claim is quite easily answered by Pope St. John XXIII's apostolic constitution *Humanae salutis*, written to explain his reasons for convoking the Council. He identified the same errors that so many of his predecessors had, even acknowledging that they had indeed created a crisis, and felt that it was an appropriate time for the Church to determine how best to address these errors. His constitution says the following:

> Today the Church is witnessing a crisis underway within society. While humanity is at the threshold of a new age, immensely serious and broad tasks await the Church, as in the most tragic periods of her history. It is a question in fact of bringing the perennial life-giving energies of the Gospel to the modern world, a world that boasts of its technical and scientific conquests but also bears the effects of a temporal order that some have wanted to reorganize by excluding God. This is why modern society is characterized by great material progress but without a corresponding advance in the moral sphere. Thence a weakening in aspirations towards the values of the spirit; thence the tendency to seek only the earthly pleasures that technological progress brings so easily within the reach of all; thence also a quite new and

disturbing fact: the existence of a militant atheism operating all over the world.[1]

Vatican II was called to address an error no less serious than the ones that previous councils addressed. As the Council of Nicaea responded to the errors of Arianism, and as Trent responded to the errors of Protestantism, Vatican II responded to "militant atheism." Militant atheism may not be in the same category of theological dissent as previous errors, but it is as or more dangerous given its global consequences in a world that was more connected than ever before.

Regarding the claim that Vatican II did not issue any anathemas, we must consider the contents of the previous chapter and recall that in a world increasingly guided by materialism where divine authority held no weight, it would have been a mistake for the Church to proceed along the path of condemning or anathematizing. This was a very deliberate decision on the part of the Council. Pope John XXIII made it clear that the Church would not continue with this tactic in his opening address, in which he said, "But at the present time, the spouse of Christ...thinks she meets today's needs by explaining the validity of her doctrine more fully rather than by condemning."[2]

---

[1] "Pope John XXIII Convokes the Second Vatican Council," trans. Joseph A. Komonchak, https://jakomonchak.files.wordpress.com/2011/12/humanae-salutis.pdf

[2] "*Gaudet Mater Ecclesia*: Pope John's Opening Speech to the Council," trans. Joseph A. Komonchak, https://jakomonchak.files.wordpress.com/2012/10/john-xxiii-opening-speech.pdf

Writing about his experience of participating in the Council, Joseph Ratzinger (the future Pope Benedict XVI) offered some very salient observations that connect this question to the morality of obligation and to the Council's intentions. He wrote, "There had been from the beginning only two kinds of doctrinal pronouncements—the creed of obligation and the anathema of negation. Both kinds of pronouncement made sense only within the realm of faith; they were based on faith's claim to authority. Since the beginning of the modern era there had been increasingly smaller circles of people ready to bow to the authority of the teaching Church." The Council intended to "replace authoritative imperatives with the proclamation of the Gospel—thus opening up the faith to the non-believer and abdicating all claim to authority other than the intrinsic authority of God's truth, manifesting itself to the hearer of the message."[3]

Considering the state of the world in the 1960s when the Council began and the fractured relationship between the spiritual and the temporal at that time, the Church knew that it would have been useless to issue a series of anathemas in her attempts to proclaim the message of the Gospel to the world. People were already abandoning the Church in droves, and she was progressively losing her influence as the world continued to succumb to secularism. Faith's claim to authority was weaker than it ever had been and would have only invited scorn and ridicule if the Church had tried to forbid the laity from assenting to certain propositions. As Ratzinger also wrote, the Council's objective was to "provide positive care for the man of today who has been told for too long what is false and what he may

---

[3] Joseph Ratzinger, *Theological Highlights of Vatican II* (Mahwah; Paulist Press, 1966), 224-225.

not do. Modern man really wishes to hear what is true. He has, indeed, not heard enough truth, enough of the positive message of faith for our own time, enough of what the faith has to say to our age."[4]

Despite this very wise decision by the Church, traditionalists claim that since no proclamation of Vatican II held explicitly authoritative weight, and since the Council was described as "pastoral," as if its decrees were no more than suggestions or helpful guides, the faithful are free to disregard them if they wish. They also claim that since the Council did not declare anything related to faith and morals, and avoided issuing any dogmatic statements, it only addressed matters of discipline and therefore was not strictly binding on the faithful. This is meant to somehow evade stating the conclusion that the Church has indeed erred—that since the Council was not doctrinal and therefore, in their judgment, not guided by the Holy Spirit, it could in fact issue error.

It is true that Pope St. Paul VI described Vatican II as "pastoral," but traditionalists often leave out some very crucial context when citing this. They use the first half of the quote, wherein Paul VI said, "Given the Council's pastoral character, it avoided pronouncing, in an extraordinary manner, dogmas endowed with the note of infallibility." However, he added, "But it [the Council] has invested its teachings with the authority of the supreme ordinary magisterium, which ordinary magisterium is so obviously authentic that *it must be accepted with docility and sincerity by all the faithful*, according to

---

[4] Ibid., 45.

the mind of the Council as expressed in the nature and aims of the individual documents."[5]

There is no question that the Holy See intended for the reforms of the Council to be binding on all the faithful. Surely, none of the Council fathers and bishops (over two thousand of them) would have expected their participation in the largest gathering in the Church's history to be for mere recommendations. The logistics of Vatican II were notoriously difficult; would any bishop have agreed to participate and be drawn into a multi-year commitment if they had known its results would be optional? For that matter, would Pope John XXIII have proceeded with convening a council of such magnitude to simply issue some helpful advice? No doubt his subordinates would not have been pleased if they arrived and then learned his true intentions.

The position that it was only disciplinary has also been refuted, and quite vehemently, by Pope Bl. Pius IX. In his encyclical *Quartus supra*, he wrote, "But the neo-schismatics say that it was not a case of doctrine but of discipline, so the name and prerogatives of Catholics cannot be denied to those who object. [...] We do not doubt that you know well how vain and worthless this evasion is."[6] His encyclical *Quanta cura*, to which the Syllabus of Errors was appended, also condemns the "audacity" of those who, "not enduring sound doctrine," declare that one may disobey a declaration from the Holy See "whose object is declared to concern the Church's general good

---

[5] "Vatican II FAQs," Word on Fire. https://www.wordonfire.org/vatican-ii-faq/#pastoral

[6] Pius IX, *Quartus supra* (1873), Papal Encyclicals Online, https://www.papalencyclicals.net/pius09/p9quartu.htm

and her rights and discipline, so only it does not touch the dogmata of faith and morals." The pontiff notes "how grievously this is opposed to the Catholic dogma of the full power given from God by Christ our Lord Himself to the Roman Pontiff of feeding, ruling and guiding the Universal Church."[7]

Consider the implications of this position. If the faithful could licitly reject disciplinary decisions, why could they not reject any practice the Church has enforced? What is preventing them from dictating their own regulations for fasting, or from deciding for themselves which feast days were of a certain class and required attendance at Mass? What is stopping clerics from using previous missals or breviaries if they so choose? All the everyday practices in the life of the Church are within the realm of "discipline," yet nobody is free to dispute these. Why, then, would they be free to reject the declarations of a council, which is of tremendously higher importance in the life of the Church?

The very glaring accusation that the Church has erred must also be addressed. The SSPX makes this very clear: "The Second Vatican Council introduced Modernist errors into the Church leading to a grave post-conciliar crisis."[8] What are these "Modernist errors" they refer to? They are 1) religious freedom, 2) ecumenism, and 3) collegiality, often referred to in traditionalist circles as the equivalent of the French Revolution's "liberte, egalite, fraternite." Is it possible for

---

[7] Pius IX, *Quanta cura* (1864), Papal Encyclicals Online, https://www.papalencyclicals.net/pius09/p9quanta.htm

[8] "Responding to false accusations," SSPX website. https://sspx.org/en/responding-to-false-accusations

the Church to officially promulgate positive error and contradict her own teachings from the past?

Yet again, Bl. Pope Pius IX, so hailed by the traditionalists for issuing the Syllabus of Errors, has directly refuted this. His encyclical *Etsi multa*, addressing the "Old Catholics" who broke away from the Church after Vatican I when they refused to accept the dogma of papal infallibility, says the following: "Incredibly, they boldly affirm that the Roman Pontiff and all the bishops, the priests and the people conjoined with him in the unity of faith and communion fell into heresy when they approved and professed the definitions of the Ecumenical Vatican Council. Therefore they deny also the indefectibility of the Church and blasphemously declare that... its visible Head and the bishops have erred."[9]

It must be asked—how does this statement differ from the position of the traditionalists today? Do they not also hold that the pope and the bishops of the world have erred when they approved and professed the definitions of Vatican II? This would have some very serious ramifications, not only for the Church, but also for the prelates who gave their assent to these "contradictions." Take, for example, the traditionalists' accusation that Vatican II's declaration on religious freedom in *Dignitatis humanae* directly contradicts Pope St. Pius X's decrees against Modernism in his encyclicals *Pascendi dominici gregis* and *Lamentabili sane*.[10] This would imply that

---

[9] Pius IX, *Etsi multa* (1873), Papal Encyclicals Online, https://www.papalencyclicals.net/pius09/p9etsimu.htm

[10] "Vatican II Council: A Much Needed Discussion," SSPX website. https://sspx.org/en/vatican-ii-council-much-needed-discussion

ninety-seven percent of the world's bishops voted in favor of positive error (2308 for and 70 against), which was then solemnly promulgated by the Pope himself. This would also mean that the entire Catholic hierarchy had excommunicated themselves from the Church, per Pope Pius X's declaration in *Praestantia scripturae:*

> [W]e do by our apostolic authority repeat and confirm both that decree of the Supreme Sacred Congregation and those encyclical letters of ours, adding the penalty of excommunication against their contradictors, and this we declare and decree that should anybody, which may God forbid, be so rash as to defend any one of the propositions, opinions or teachings condemned in these documents he falls, ipso facto, under the censure contained under the chapter "Docentes" of the constitution "Apostolicae Sedis," which is the first among the excommunications *latae sententiae,* simply reserved to the Roman Pontiff.[11]

Are our church leaders so incompetent that they 1) did not know what these previous declarations said or meant, 2) did not understand that the new declarations seemed to conflict with them, or 3) proceeded to vote in the affirmative regardless? Or, being guided by the Holy Spirit in a general council, do our shepherds have a higher understanding of the theological and ecclesiastical subtleties than

---

[11] Pius X, *Praestantia scripturae* (1907), Papal Encyclicals Online, https://www.papalencyclicals.net/pius10/p10prasc.htm (emphasis in original)

the sheep do? As St. Francis de Sales wrote, "[I]f the legitimate assembly of the pastors and heads of the Church could once be surprised by error, how would the word of the master be verified: *The gates of hell shall not prevail against it*?"[12]

Not to mention, if the Church can err and has indeed erred, who is to say this has not happened before? Who is to say it will not happen again? How can we trust any judgment she has issued if the faithful could identify errors when her shepherds have not? How can we know whether any of her previous declarations were infected with errors? Are any of the faithful still living in the grip of positive error declared by popes of the last century? A dire situation if there ever was one, and one that would require an immediate resolution, as the salvation of souls is at stake!

Yet even though the charges brought by the traditionalists against the Council are incompatible with Catholic tradition, they maintain that as long as the Council stands, the crisis will continue. The question then becomes a more practical one. Is it possible to redact a council's declarations, or even an entire council? Can it be removed from the historical record, and can the Church wind back time to pretend that it never happened? Most reasonable traditionalists will agree that most of the content of Vatican II's documents is acceptable, and it is just a small percentage that is problematic. Certainly, one could not read the documents and say that they are entirely compromised; often it amounts to one phrase or passage that they take issue with, such as the ever-debated "*subsistit in*."

---

[12] Francis de Sales, *The Catholic Controversy* (1886; Charlotte, TAN Books, 1989), 163 (emphasis in original)

Is it realistic to think that the confusion in the Church today would be resolved by editing a couple of words or phrases in documents that most Catholics have not even read, nor care to read? Was the Church secure in her tradition before the Council and completely upended by a few "ambiguous" words or phrases? We cannot pretend that the crisis of faith is contingent on several statements that some people believe to be unclear. The Church has already issued clarifications on those passages that generated controversy; should she keep doing so until everyone is satisfied? Often, a perfectly acceptable clarification can be found in the documents themselves. For example, *Dignitatis humanae* explicitly states, "Religious freedom, in turn, which men demand as necessary to fulfill their duty to worship God, has to do with immunity from coercion in civil society. Therefore it leaves untouched traditional Catholic doctrine on the moral duty of men and societies toward the true religion and toward the one Church of Christ."[13] One could hardly accuse the Council of "watering down" the Church's integrity after reading this passage.

And how ought we to measure the acceptability of a certain clarification or redaction? Might it be acceptable for some, but not others? Are certain statements orthodox enough for one bishop but not his brother bishop? Why is one traditionalist bishop right or wrong when he claims that one sentence is ambiguous when another might not acknowledge the same ambiguity? If each person could individually determine whether the pronouncements of the magisterium

---

[13] Paul VI, Declaration on Religious Freedom *Dignitatis humanae*, Vatican Archive, https://www.vatican.va/archive/hist_councils/ii_vatican_council/documents/vat-ii_decl_19651207_dignitatis-humanae_en.html

were to his or her satisfaction, or whether or not they mitigated a crisis of faith, does this not place individual subjectivity over the authority of the Church? When is the matter *objectively* settled?

St. Francis de Sales offers a very applicable musing on this very topic; one could almost think this was written within the last few decades, and directed at those who object to the Second Vatican Council's declarations.

> The Councils, after the fullest consultation, when the test has been made by the holy touchstone of the Word of God, decide and define some article. If after all this another test has to be tried before their determination is received, will not another also be wanted? Who will not want to apply his test, and whenever will the matter be settled? [...] And who shall stop another from asking as much, in order to see if the Council's test has been properly tried? And why not a third to know if the second is faithful? —and then a fourth, to test the third? Everything must be done over again, and posterity will never trust antiquity but will go ever turning upside down the holiest articles of the faith in the wheel of their understandings. [...] But, I beseech you, if the test as applied by a General Council be not enough to settle the minds of men, how shall the authority of some nobody be able to do it?[14]

Placing one's own interpretation of the documents above the Church introduces subjectivity that can only further the confusion.

---

[14] Sales, *The Catholic Controversy*, 166-167.

To whom can we have recourse if not the Church? If she is wrong, who is right? Can a single bishop have a perfect grasp of tradition that the magisterium somehow overlooked? Private judgment against the declarations of a council has never been and cannot be the answer. In a letter to Archbishop Lefebvre on July 28, 1987, then-Cardinal Ratzinger said the following to Archbishop Lefebvre: "By giving a personal interpretation of the texts of the magisterium, you would paradoxically give an example of this Liberalism which you fight so strongly, and would act contrarily to the goal you pursue."[15]

It would set a very dangerous precedent if an event of such magnitude and its declarations would always have the possibility of being completely erased if its "fruits" were not immediately discernible. How could we ever have faith in the gathering of the Church's shepherds, especially in the future when there will only be more bishops and larger gatherings? On what kind of unsteady footing would that put the Church? How would that make her look to outsiders, when her power has already been so diminished in the eyes of the world? The past hundred years have been eroding the Church's divine authority, and in trying to re-establish itself as an institution with truth to give to the world, would it not be a kind of ecclesiastical suicide to admit to such a catastrophic mistake as proclaiming positive error and basing all the Church's activity on this

---

[15] Joseph Ratzinger, Letter to Archbishop Lefebvre, July 28, 1987, *Archbishop Lefebvre and the Vatican.* https://www.sspxasia.com/Documents/Archbishop-Lefebvre/Archbishop_Lefebvre_and_the_Vatican/Part_I/1987-07_28.htm

error? How could anyone, especially potential converts, have confidence in the Church? She would lose all credibility if she admitted to being wrong after such a historically significant event.

Consider the voting totals of the Council. Averaging the votes across all sixteen documents, the Council's declarations were passed with a ninety-eight and a half percent approval rate. If the documents did indeed contain errors, this would reveal the alarming fact that almost the entire Church was already compromised before any reforms were implemented, and less than two percent of all the world's bishops had the fortitude to vote against texts that introduced error, confusion, and crisis into the Church. Would this not prove that the Tridentine form of the Mass and "pre-conciliar Catholicism," which all those bishops celebrated and maintained, had not been able to withstand those errors in the preceding decades (or centuries)? What would have happened if no council was ever called? The faithful would have been stumbling along in spiritual darkness, led by shepherds who were outwardly "traditional" but interiorly nefarious.

While it is completely understandable to have hesitations or questions about the Council, the traditionalists' position does not yield a satisfactory resolution. They believe that their interpretation is the correct one, and the Church simply must admit that she made a colossal mistake. But this completely undermines the magisterium of the Church and places ultimate authority in the hands of individuals, any one of whom could demand that their interpretation was the most "traditional." If the Church did (or could) admit to promoting error, and edited her declarations to satisfy one group, why not do it again for the demands of another? Fr. Denis Crouan wrote that rallying to the traditionalists "would create anarchy, since it would subject the Pope to any number of pressure groups who would claim to be right in opposing him. [...] If the Pope were to acknowledge the 'errors' committed since Vatican II, that would validate the Modernist theories, for instance, that acts of disobedience are sometimes legitimate, and that the Pope has only a relative authority."[16]

All too often, especially in America, which was founded on the spirit of revolution, Catholics can succumb to the erroneous idea that exerting enough pressure on authority figures or persisting in resistance long enough will motivate the authorities to acquiesce to their requests. A great danger exists of our seeing the Church in the same way we see our government, merely as elected officials who can be "bought and sold," rather than as shepherds who foster the care of souls. It is most certainly true that they can abuse that power for their own personal gain, but as Pope Pius XII said in *Mystici Corporis Christi*, "if at times there appears in the Church something that indicates the weakness of our human nature, it should not be attributed to her juridical constitution, but rather to that regrettable inclination to evil found in each individual, which its Divine Founder permits even at times in the most exalted members of His Mystical Body, for the purpose of testing the virtue of the Shepherds

---

[16] Denis Crouan, *The History and the Future of the Roman Liturgy*, trans. Michael Miller (San Francisco; Ignatius Press, 2005) 213 (Ignatius Press Reprint edition).

no less than of the flocks, and that all may increase the merit of their Christian faith."[17]

Neither the Council nor its central declarations will be redacted. Having been ratified by the Holy See, confirmed and promoted by four subsequent popes, and acting as the source for all the Church's efforts at evangelization for the past 60 years, it is impossible that they can simply be reversed. How could the Church possibly root out every reference to the Council in all its literature, catechetical programs, theology, and everything else that has come from it? The only option is to forge ahead. Pope Benedict XVI had some very direct words on this matter: "Was the Council a wrong road that we must now retrace if we are to save the Church? The voices of those who say that it was are becoming louder and their followers more numerous. [...] Without a doubt, they represent a sectarian zealotry that is the antithesis of Catholicity. We cannot resist them too firmly."[18]

---

[17] Pius XII, *Mystici Corporis Christi*, (1943), Vatican Archive, https://www.vatican.va/content/pius-xii/en/encyclicals/documents/hf_p-xii_enc_29061943_mystici-corporis-christi.html

[18] Joseph Ratzinger, *Principles of Catholic Theology: Building Stones for a Fundamental Theology*, trans. Sr. Mary Frances McCarthy, S.N.D. (San Francisco: Ignatius Press, 1987), 389-390.

3.

The Liturgical Reform

There is a fundamental misunderstanding in traditionalist circles that the Mass as it was celebrated before Vatican II was not in need of change. This idea is especially promoted by those who are fleeing irreverent or casual liturgies and happen to discover a Latin Mass. Why, they ask, was something so rich and reverent suppressed for something that to them seems so banal? What exactly was wrong with the Mass that necessitated such an overhaul, and how did we pivot from Latin, incense, and Gregorian chant to felt banners, clapping, and casual liturgical celebrations? To the traditionalists, it is clear; the Novus Ordo Missae, often described as a "Protestant Mass" (or worse), was simply a mistake, and it must be discarded. To them, only a return to the missal of 1962 will generate the reverence and devotion that is admittedly lacking in many parishes.

In response to this, defenders of the liturgical reform will often cite their own anecdotal evidence. They remind the traditionalists that before the Council, Mass was often rushed (reportedly celebrated in fifteen minutes), the Latin was mangled and mumbled, communion was distributed at intervals throughout Mass instead of at the proper time, and the people in the pews simply observed and did not know what was happening or why, content to simply fulfill their Sunday obligation. For advocates of the Novus Ordo Missae, this is clear proof that something was clearly amiss and needed to be reformed.

Both sides have legitimate grievances, but both miss the bigger picture. Why, before the Council, did priests mangle the Latin, skip prayers, and rush through the Mass? Why, after the Council, did priests feel it was acceptable to change the rubrics and allow liturgical practices that varied from imprudent to outright sacrilegious?

We again must consider the mindset of functionality that had overtaken the world and was seeping into the Church in the 20th century. As Joseph Ratzinger wrote, humanity had been reorienting its perspective toward making things "functional in the service of man" for decades or even centuries before the liturgical reform, and now "no longer approaches the world from the viewpoint of contemplation and wonder[.]" As a result, "religious mystery largely vanishes from things because this mystery cannot be methodologically examined."[1]

Whether the world's functional outlook on reality influenced the Church's understanding of her central mysteries, or the morality of obligation unfortunately coincided with this change, the fact is that the religious mystery imbued in the sacraments had become stifled by ritualism over the last several centuries. The de-emphasis of Scripture in favor of private prayer that also occurred during this time may have been another contributing factor. The Eucharistic liturgy had become "a collection of rites scrupulously executed to insure validity and sacramental efficacy,"[2] as Fr. Marcel Metzger wrote, and was not understood as the universal prayer of the Church, but as a series of rubrics that imparted grace on attendants.

---

[1] Ratzinger, *Theological Highlights of Vatican II*, 232.

[2] Marcel Metzger, *History of the Liturgy*, trans. Madeleine Beaumont (Collegeville; The Liturgical Press, 1997), 133.

The liturgy had also become overshadowed by the practice of private devotions, some of which had crept into the liturgical celebration itself. When the missal was codified in the Middle Ages, it was no longer possible to incorporate regional practices into the liturgy (a crucial part of the "organic development" so often cited by the traditionalists), so the spiritual lives of the people began to be nourished by devotions. It is worth noting that these devotions were often "measurable," consisting of a certain number of repetitions, or prayers to be said on certain days, or a specific indulgence attached to a particular practice. Piety was no longer about mystery; it, too, had become "functional." The liturgy, a public act by its very nature (from the Greek *leitourgia*, meaning "public work" or "work of the people"), had become supplanted as the external expression of Catholic piety by a collection of private acts on the part of the people. Even devotions that the priest performed made their way into the liturgy, such as the Prayers at the Foot of the Altar and the Last Gospel, both of which originally served as private prayers for the priest to say while he vested and de-vested for Mass.

Knowing the cultural factors that had influenced the mentality of the people (and therefore of the priests), and the rubrical rigor of liturgical celebrations (which certainly had its merits, but also unfortunately did not permit for legitimate development besides top-down decrees from the Holy See), it is perhaps easier to see why the old form of the Mass had become, as Ratzinger so boldly put it, "a rigid, fixed, and firmly encrusted system" that was "ultimately doomed to internal decay."[3] The liturgy and the sacraments had become less about participating in the *mysterium fidei*, the "mystery of faith," and more about how they could serve the people by bestowing grace or by fulfilling a specific function.

A self-centered world had influenced Catholic spirituality as well, and when mystery was diminished, the Mass gave way to the often-referenced liturgical abuses that occurred before the Council. If nobody knew Latin, why not mumble it or skip prayers? The people would not know the difference. If they were busy with their rosary in the pew, why not rush through the silent prayers? The people would not be able to tell. If receiving the Eucharist was simply another rubric in a collection, why not administer it throughout Mass, since that was more convenient? This spirit of "functional spirituality" was already festering before the Church finally addressed it in the 1960s.

The Church knew this topic was pressing, and the liturgical reform was the first topic discussed at Vatican II. It was not something that had suddenly been proposed before the Council; its roots go back to the late 19th century, and it was encouraged by figures such as Romano Guardini and Dom Odo Casel, and by popes such as Pius X and Pius XII. Discoveries of historical texts such as the *Didache* and research into liturgical practices of the past were becoming more common during this time, and the Church was beginning to recover the sense of communal worship as a Body rather than as a collection of acts or congregations.

---

[3] Ratzinger, *Theological Highlights of Vatican II*, 131.

There is no question that the codified missal had suffered from certain setbacks which required attention. For as grandiose and stately as the Mass was, a close inspection revealed elements which had over time been layered on top of each other, resulting in rubrics that were weighed down by what Joseph Ratzinger described as "superfluous accretions of purely historical value."[4] The most glaring of these was the disconnect between the priest and the faithful, stemming from the practice of private Masses. A sung Mass essentially had two separate liturgies occurring parallel to each other, in which the priest would intone a prayer, then whisper the remainder of it quietly and sit down while waiting for the choir to finish chanting it. This led to the duplication of many prayers, one said by the priest and the altar servers and another by the people in sung form, and unfortunately perpetuated the disconnect between the celebrant and the congregation.

There was also a multiplication of gestures such as Signs of the Cross, genuflections, and kissing of the altar that had become somewhat excessive, presenting the "risk of sliding into an exaggerated sentimentality,"[5] as Fr. Denis Crouan wrote. Other inconsistencies such as an *"Oremus"* ("Let us pray") that was not actually followed by a prayer, or the dismissal that was then followed by the Last Gospel, or Offertory prayers that were too anticipatory of the Eucharistic Prayer with their reference to an "unspotted host" and "chalice of salvation," showed that this was a ritual which had maintained an impressive appearance and a rich history but had also accumulated

---

[4] Ibid., 133.

[5] Denis Crouan, *The Liturgy Betrayed*, trans. Marc Sebanc (San Francisco; Ignatius Press, 2000), 45.

various prayers and gestures whose original meaning had been lost over time. As Joseph Ratzinger wrote, "The essence of the ancient Christian liturgy in the texts was no longer visible in the overgrowth of pious additions."[6] He also compared it to a fresco that had been "preserved from damage, but it had been almost completely overlaid with whitewash by later generations," and that the earliest form of the liturgy was "largely concealed beneath instructions for and forms of private prayer."[7]

Thus we can see that the "missal of Pius V" or "Tridentine missal," as it is known in traditionalist circles, is hardly the pinnacle of liturgical expression. While it is a valuable part of our Catholic heritage and certainly ought to be respected and appreciated, the Church recognized that in our present time, change was necessary.

The reform of the liturgy was about much more than editing a few prayers or changing some of the rubrics. It would not be enough to simply permit the readings in the vernacular or remove a handful of minor gestures. A true renewal of our understanding of the liturgy was necessary to bring the central mystery to the forefront. Ratzinger further wrote, "[T]he necessary revamping could not take place simply through purely stylistic modifications, but also required a new theology of divine worship. Otherwise the renewal would be no more than superficial,"[8] One could hardly expect that the Church would attempt to face the oncoming wave of secularism by maintaining the same understanding of divine worship that the

---

[6] Ratzinger, *Theological Highlights of Vatican II*, 129.

[7] Joseph Ratzinger, *The Spirit of the Liturgy*, trans. John Saward (San Francisco; Ignatius Press, 2000), 7-8.

[8] Ibid., 133.

people currently held. Consider the following stipulations from *Sacrosanctum concilium*, the constitution on the Sacred Liturgy.

> 30. To promote active participation, the people should be encouraged to take part by means of acclamations, responses, psalmody, antiphons, and songs, as well as by actions, gestures, and bodily attitudes. And at the proper times all should observe a reverent silence.
>
> 34. The rites should be distinguished by a noble simplicity; they should be short, clear, and unencumbered by useless repetitions; they should be within the people's powers of comprehension, and normally should not require much explanation.
>
> 50. The rite of the Mass is to be revised in such a way that the intrinsic nature and purpose of its several parts, as also the connection between them, may be more clearly manifested, and that devout and active participation by the faithful may be more easily achieved.
>
> For this purpose the rites are to be simplified, due care being taken to preserve their substance; elements which, with the passage of time, came to be duplicated, or were added with but little advantage, are now to be discarded; other elements which have suffered injury through accidents of history are now to be restored to the vigor which they had in the days of the holy Fathers, as may seem useful or necessary.
>
> 51. The treasures of the bible are to be opened up more lavishly, so that richer fare may be provided for the faithful

at the table of God's word. In this way a more representative portion of the holy scriptures will be read to the people in the course of a prescribed number of years.

The constitution also described the "active participation" referenced in section 30 and 50 as "the aim to be considered before all else," calling it "the primary and indispensable source from which the faithful are to derive the true Christian spirit[.]"[9] The Church understood well that the faithful could not content themselves with being "strangers or silent spectators,"[10] but must be engaged with the liturgy in the proper way, whether that be vocally or silently.

Almost every single bishop present at the Council voted in the affirmative on the reforms proposed by *Sacrosanctum concilium* (2,147 for, and 4 against). Looking at this, one cannot help but be skeptical of the protests about the Latin Mass being the "Mass of the Ages," or the appeals to *Quo primum*, Pope Pius V's papal bull promulgating the "Tridentine missal," which contains an often-misunderstood clause about its being a perpetual order. (Why did no bishop think to remind his brother bishops or the Pope of this clause if *Quo primum* did forbid changes like the traditionalists claim?) The mind of the Church clearly believed that something was lacking in the liturgy, and that a reform of some significance was due.

---

[9] Second Vatican Council, Constitution on the Sacred Liturgy *Sacrosanctum Concilium* (1963), Vatican Archive, https://www.vatican.va/archive/hist_councils/ii_vatican_council/documents/vat-ii_const_19631204_sacrosanctum-concilium_en.html

[10] Ibid.

Certain elements that had been part of the liturgy since its earliest days and which the Church now saw as once more beneficial were reintroduced, such as the Prayer of the Faithful after the Creed, the Sign of Peace (which, it may surprise some to learn, was actually part of the Roman rite for many centuries), the audible recitation of the Canon, and others. The lectionary was vastly expanded to include more Scripture passages, and a second reading before the Gospel was added. The necessary connection between the priest and the people was restored by arranging the prayers so that they formed an exchange between the two. The end result was a revised missal that did indeed simplify the rites, remove superfluous elements, and restore various ancient practices.

An excellent example of the "noble simplicity" envisioned by the Council is the revision to the prayer during the distribution of communion. In the old form of the Mass, the priest would say *"Corpus Domini nostri Jesu Christi custodiat animam tuam in vitam aeternam, amen"*[11] to each communicant. It is not difficult to see how such a prayer, while beautiful, could benefit from a revision. It became all too easy for priests to mumble their way through this prayer, often skipping several words or moving on to the next communicant before they had finished it. The revised rite of Mass simply directs the priest to say "The Body of Christ" to each communicant as he presents the host, to which they respond "Amen" before receiving the Eucharist. This was a practice dating back to the early Church, and expresses a simple yet profound act—the minister of

---

[11] "The Body of Our Lord Jesus Christ preserve your soul unto life everlasting. Amen."

the Church declaring the truth of the Eucharist, and the people professing their assent to this truth before receiving it.

Qualms or disagreements with certain elements of the reform are understandable. It was undoubtedly ambitious and may have succumbed to a certain eagerness that to some might have given the appearance of shaking the foundations of Catholic worship. But the fact of the matter remains, the bishops of the world universally agreed that this was necessary, and a reform of this scope could not occur through organic development or gradual change. (One wonders how organic development could occur if the missal was codified and was not allowed to develop except by way of papal declarations.) The movement that resisted changes to the Mass showed its hand (a frankly disingenuous one) when it rejected the reforms only *after* being dissatisfied with the results.

The abuses of the liturgy in the years following the Council are certainly not to be downplayed. Traditionalists are right to deplore the scandals caused by improvisations, and these must be curbed if the liturgical reform is to yield its intended fruit. Similarly, proper implementation of *Sacrosanctum concilium* must be prioritized, and liturgical elements like the Latin language, Gregorian chant, and sacred art ought to be more present, as the document stipulates. But can the Council or the missal be blamed when they allow for no such mishandling of the Church's most sacred prayer? *Sacrosanctum concilium* stated, "Therefore no other person, even if he be a priest, may add, remove, or change anything in the liturgy on his own authority." We can hardly blame the Council when it very expressly forbade what came to dominate the vast majority of parishes in the Western world.

The abuses of the liturgy stem from the same deep-seated errors that the world had faced for centuries, mostly a desire to make things functional. This is why some priests had no qualms about inserting practices after Vatican II that appealed to their own personal tastes or to what they thought the people wanted. Before the Council, the crisis expressed itself as rushed, sloppy, or otherwise deficient celebrations which saw little purpose in the "archaic" language and gestures; afterward, it expressed itself as an absolute free-for-all, in which priests cited the "spirit of Vatican II" (i.e., "change") as a justification for all improvisations according to what might satisfy their "audience." When the mystery of the liturgy was obscured and the externals were highlighted, attempts would naturally be made to reorganize the externals as an end in and of themselves, always trying novel things when one inevitably failed to produce spiritual fulfillment. But these will only be empty gestures if the people do not understand what their worship actually consists of. As Pope Pius XII wrote regarding the sacraments and the Eucharistic sacrifice, "[I]f they are to produce their proper effect, it is absolutely necessary that our hearts be properly disposed to receive them."[12] Hearts that had turned toward the modern age had less and less room for spiritual pursuits.

In this same vein, however, it must be acknowledged that a simple return to the older form of the missal is not the answer to the current crisis. There is a common belief in traditionalist circles that the "Latin Mass" is a bulwark against heresy, that it inherently has

---

[12] Pius XII, *Mediator Dei* (1947), Vatican Archive, https://www.vatican.va/content/pius-xii/en/encyclicals/documents/hf_p-xii_enc_2011-1947_mediator-dei.html

more graces attached to it by virtue of its longer collection of prayers and gestures, and that one's faith is significantly more likely to be nourished or even retained as long as one is attending this form of the Mass. This implies some sort of objective, measurable quantity of grace to certain rubrics or prayers, displaying the "functional spirituality" that necessitated a reform in the first place, and ignores the fact that this form of the Mass was celebrated during the time when the crisis began. As James Likoudis and Kenneth Whitehead state in their book *The Pope, The Council, and The Mass:*

> The "Mass of Saint Pius V," with all its admirable features, which Paul VI and others have often remarked on, was no barrier to the doctrinal deviations that have been the true cause of the decline of Catholic faith and practice in the Church in the twentieth century. The root causes for the present "crisis of faith" and "crisis of authority"—crises which affect both Church and society—lie far deeper than which Mass is being celebrated, and it would be a profound mistake to think otherwise.[13]

The idea that a certain form of the Roman rite is imbued with inherent orthodoxy that protects against error is simply false. One need only examine the historical context surrounding the Church in previous centuries to understand this. The older form of the Mass

---

[13] James Likoudis and Kenneth D. Whitehead, *The Pope, The Council, and The Mass* (Steubenville, Ohio: Emmaus Road Publishing, 2006), 154.

was being celebrated at the time that the errors of Protestantism began spreading throughout Europe; errors so dire that the Church had to convene a council to address them. Since then, the Church has suffered through the heresies of Gallicanism, Jansenism, and others, as well as the schism of the Old Catholics following the First Vatican Council. Not to mention, this form of the Mass was being celebrated during the early 20th century when Modernism was identified and so strongly condemned, and when the Church subsequently adopted a firmly defensive stance to reinforce its condemnations, issuing such things as the Index of Forbidden Books and the Syllabus of Errors.

It is a mistake to think that a return to the missal of 1962 will solve the crisis of the liturgy. The rampant liturgical abuse of the last several decades has primarily occurred in Western countries that were most affected by materialism, scientific progress, and agnosticism. Priests who subjected their congregations to these abuses had previously celebrated the "Latin Mass" and were formed in the seminaries of the early 20th century. Clearly, the issue runs deeper. The Church, in her wisdom, has permitted continued usage of the 1962 missal under certain circumstances, but the older form of the Mass does not fix the root of the problem; it simply provides temporary relief from the problem's most noticeable effects such as irreverence. No rubrics or prayers will "fix" the problem of widespread unbelief. The rejection of authority and an inclination toward functionality are responsible, and a certain language or certain prayers cannot repel that. What is necessary is a true rediscovery of what worship consists of and what our part in it is.

PART II

TRADITIONALIST DEFENSES

4.

Mission

Mission is at the very heart of the Church, just as it is the very essence of her founder. Jesus, the eternal Word and the eternal "sending forth" of the Father, is "the living source of all ecclesiastical mission," as St. Francis de Sales wrote, and has "a mission so authentic that it comprises the communication of the same essence."[1] Jesus makes it very clear that He came to earth, not of His own accord, but sent from an authority higher than He, reminding His followers that He has been "sent" by the Father on quite a number of occasions— more than thirty times just in the Gospel of John alone! For example, John 5:24: "Truly, truly, I say to you, he who hears my word and believes him who sent me, has eternal life[.]" Or in John 8:18: "I bear witness to myself, and the Father who sent me bears witness to me." Yet another example is in John 12:44: "And Jesus cried out and said, "He who believes in me, believes not in me but in him who sent me."

Our Lord's meaning is unmistakable. He did not come by His own power but came to carry out the will of the One who sent Him, a commission He then passed to the apostles. The whole message of the Gospel is contingent on being taught and spread by those who are delegated by Christ for this task, in what is known as the Great Commission. The word "apostle" derives from the Greek *apostolos*, which literally translated means "one who is sent," or "messenger." This word is derived from the verb *apostellein*; *apo* meaning "away

---

[1] Sales, *The Catholic Controversy*, 10

from," and *stellein*, "to send." Jesus entrusted the twelve apostles with the mission of bringing His teaching to the world when He said, "As the Father has sent me, even so I send you," (Jn 20:21) and entrusted them with His very Body and Blood in His command to "take…eat" and "do this."

The mission of Jesus is then transmitted through the Mass. As the Catechism explains, the Mass earns its name from the Latin *missa* "because the liturgy in which the mystery of salvation is accomplished concludes with the sending forth (*missio*) of the faithful, so that they may fulfill God's will in their daily lives."[2] The Latin dismissal of the older form of the Mass, "*Ite, missa est,*" is often rendered as "Go forth, the Mass is ended," but it literally translates to "Go, it is the sending." The Mass is the sending of the people out into the world after being nourished with the Bread of Life and the Word of the Lord, so that they can bring Jesus and His teachings to others.

Mission is an essential element of the Church. God the Father sent his Son, the Son sent the apostles, the apostles sent their successors (the bishops), their successors continue to send their delegates (the priests), and their delegates continue to send the faithful out into the world at every Mass in order to fulfill the same mission that was given to the apostles: "Go therefore and make disciples of all nations." As Joseph Ratzinger wrote, mission "has a sacramental basis" and "involves being united in a concrete sense with the Body of

---

[2] Catechism of the Catholic Church, 2nd ed. 2022, n. 1332

Christ, which was sacrificed and is living eternally in the Resurrection."[3] As Jesus the Incarnate Word came to earth with a mission, the Body of Christ here on earth continues that mission.

Let us return to the previously mentioned verses in the Gospel of John to understand the importance of mission in the life of the Church. Reading Jesus' references to being sent by the Father, one will frequently see a reminder from Jesus himself that even He, the Son of God, must be authorized by a higher authority to carry out a mission. Think about Jesus Christ, the Son of God, saying very plainly, "I do nothing of my own accord." A few examples are as follows:

"*I can do nothing on my own authority*; as I hear, I judge; and my judgment is just, because I seek not my own will but the will of him who sent me." (Jn 5:30)

So Jesus said, "When you have lifted up the Son of man, then you will know that I am he, and that *I do nothing on my own authority* but speak thus as the Father taught me." (Jn 8:28)

"*For I have not spoken on my own authority*; the Father who sent me has himself given me commandment what to say and what to speak." (Jn 12:49)

These words ought to strike a certain note for us. The Son of God, the Incarnate Word, is asserting that He cannot carry out the

---

[3] Ratzinger, *Pilgrim Fellowship of Faith,* 120

will of the Father on His own terms, or on His own judgment. He does not come to do what He thinks is best, or how He thinks it ought to be done. He comes in obedience and in submission to the one who has sent Him, the One who has the power to send Him.

Looking further back in the scriptures, we can see this also expressed in explicit terms in the book of Jeremiah.

> And the LORD said to me: "The prophets are prophesying lies in my name; *I did not send them*, nor did I command them or speak to them. They are prophesying to you...the deceit of their own minds." (Jer 14:14)

> Behold, I am against those who prophesy lying dreams, says the LORD, and who tell them and lead my people astray by their lies and their recklessness, *when I did not send them or charge them*; so they do not profit this people at all, says the LORD. (Jer 23:32)

> Then the word of the LORD came to Jeremiah: "Send to all the exiles, saying, 'Thus says the Lord concerning Shemai'ah of Nehel'am: *Because Shemai'ah had prophesied to you when I did not send him, [he] has made you trust in a lie[.]*'" (Jer 29:30)

The tradition of the Church is very clear; one must be sent by lawful authority to minister on behalf of the Church. A mission is no mission at all if it is self-delegated, or accepted from one who has claimed a mission for themselves. As Christ could do nothing on His

own authority, neither can any minister of the Church. In the words
of Rt. Rev. Lawrence Sheil:

> But the example of Christ himself is most certainly of the
> greatest weight to convince us that no man can legally enter
> upon the sacred ministry, except he be sent according to the
> order established by God. For if the Son of God took not
> upon him the preaching of the gospel but as sent by his eter-
> nal Father, what sacrilegious arrogance and presumption
> must it then be in men to assume to themselves this sacred
> function without a commission from any lawful authority?[4]

St. Paul reaffirms the necessity of a mission in his letter to the
Romans when he says, "But how are men to call upon him in whom
they have not believed? And how are they to believe in him of whom
they have never heard? And how are they to hear without a
preacher? *And how can men preach unless they are sent?*" (Rom
10:15)

The Baltimore Catechism, a favorite in traditionalist circles, re-
inforces this tradition in question 1004:

> Q. Can bishops, priests and other ministers of the Church
> always exercise the power they have received in Holy Or-
> ders?

---

[4] Lawrence Sheil, *The Bible Against Protestantism and for Catholicity,*
5th ed. (Boston: Donahoe, 1859), 240-241

A. Bishops, priests and other ministers of the Church cannot exercise the power they have received in Holy Orders *unless authorized and sent to do so by their lawful superiors.*[5]

The question, then, is who are the lawful superiors of traditionalist priests? The answer is, quite simply, no one. They have no lawful superiors. The vagus bishops from whom they receive their Holy Orders are merely the mechanism by which they receive their power, but these bishops have no authority to send these priests to minister anywhere. They have not been assigned as shepherds over these priests by the Holy See, nor over the people of the dioceses into which they send them. The bishops are "priest makers" without any governing authority. This was expressly condemned at Trent:

> [C]ertain bishops…being in a manner wanderers, having no fixed see, …do, by an evasion and in contempt of the law, of their own rashness choose as it were an episcopal chair in a place which is not of any diocese, and presume to mark with the clerical character, and to promote even to the sacred orders of the priesthood, any that come unto them, even though they have no commendatory letters from their own bishops, or prelates[.][6]

---

[5] The Catholic Primer, *The Catholic Primer's Reference Series: The Baltimore Catechism of 1891*, 2005, n. 1004. https://www.catechism.cc/catechisms/Baltimore_Catechism.pdf

[6] General Council of Trent: Fourteenth Session, Decree on Reformation, Chapter II, Papal Encyclicals Online, https://www.papalencyclicals.net/councils/trent/fourteenth-session.htm

Having no lawful superiors, traditionalist priests have no lawful delegation to minister anywhere and are assuming a mission onto themselves. They are doing precisely what the scriptures so strongly condemn—presuming to preach in the name of God without being sent by God. Incredibly, they dare to do what the Son of God said was impossible for Him to do. This is a very serious matter; so serious, in fact, that the Council of Trent anathematized it in Session XXIII, Chapter IV, Canon VII: "If any one saith, ...that those who have neither been rightly ordained, nor sent, by ecclesiastical and canonical power, but come from elsewhere, are lawful ministers of the word and of the sacraments; let him be anathema."[7]

This canon is vital for examining the traditionalist position. As the Council stated, not only are they in error who presume to minister without being ordained; they are equally in error who, although ordained, assume the responsibilities of a minister of God's word and His sacraments without being delegated by lawful authority. As Rev. Sebastian Smith wrote, "The power of order and the power of jurisdiction are separable and essentially distinct one from the other. This distinction is thus expressed by the Council of Trent [in Canon VII]...If solely by virtue of their ordination bishops and priests were possessed of sufficient jurisdiction, the holy synod would not have

---

[7] General Council of Trent: Twenty-Third Session, On the Sacrament of Order, Canon VII, Papal Encyclicals Online, https://www.papalencyclicals.net/councils/trent/twenty-third-session.htm

added, *nec missi sunt* [nor have been sent]."[8] Clearly the great Council does not intend to simply say that no man can claim the responsibilities of a cleric; it also says that no cleric can claim jurisdiction, or send himself, and still be considered a lawful minister of the Church. One cannot understate the gravity of this canon. The Council of Trent, held in such high esteem by traditionalists, has actually anathematized their *modus operandi*!

And this is not only condemned by Trent. In his encyclical *Graves ac diuturnae*, Pope Bl. Pius IX said that the faithful "should not have any dealings or meetings with usurping priests…who dare to exercise the duties of an ecclesiastical minister without possessing a legitimate mission," and that they should "avoid them as strangers and thieves who come only to steal, slay, and destroy."[9] He went on to exhort them "with the greatest enthusiasm to give support strongly and constantly to your legitimate shepherds who have received a legitimate mission from this Apostolic See. They watch over your souls since they will have to account to God for them."[10]

Similarly, in his encyclical "On Preaching the Word of God," Pope Benedict XV wrote the following to the bishops of the world:

> Let this then be the first law laid down: that no one on his own responsibility undertake the office of preaching. *In order to fulfill that duty everyone must have a lawful mission,*

---

[8] Sebastian Smith, *Elements of Ecclesiastical Law* (New York; Benzinger Bros., 1895), 88

[9] Pius IX, *Graves ac diuturnae* (1875), Papal Encyclicals Online, https://www.papalencyclicals.net/pius09/p9graves.htm

[10] Ibid.

and that mission can be conferred by the Bishop alone. [...]
For the man who owing to his peculiar bent of mind, or any
other cause, should choose to undertake the ministry of the
Word, finds easy access to the pulpits of our churches as to a
drill-ground where any one may practice at will. Therefore,
Venerable Brethren, it is your duty to see that such a grave
abuse should disappear, and since you will have to render to
God and to His Church an account of the manner in which
you feed your flock, allow no one to creep unbidden into the
sheepfold and to feed the sheep of Christ according to his
fancy. *Therefore let no one henceforth preach in your dioceses
except on your summons and with your approval.*[11]

The question then becomes, if they have no delegated jurisdiction, from where does their "authority" come? Their answer—from
the needs of the people, or from the "state of necessity" that permits
the people to request sacraments from any priest who is willing to
give them. Archbishop Lefebvre said that a bishop in the traditionalist situation "has no other basis for jurisdiction than that which
comes from the requests of the priests and the faithful to take care
of their souls…and who have asked him to accept the episcopacy[.]"
He also said this bishop's jurisdiction is not "territorial" but "personal," that it would have, as its source, "the duty of the faithful to
save their souls," and that "the jurisdictional authority of the bishop

---

[11] Benedict XV, *Humani generis redemptionem* (1917), Vatican Archive, https://www.vatican.va/content/benedict-xv/en/encyclicals/docu-
ments/hf_ben-xv_enc_15061917_humani-generis-redemptionem.html

does not come from a Roman nomination, but from the necessity of the salvation of souls[.]"[12]

Yet again, this position has been denounced in no uncertain terms by the Council of Trent. Session XXIII, Chapter IV says the following: "[A]ll those who, *being only called and instituted by the people*, or by the civil power and magistrate, ascend to the exercise of [priestly] ministrations, *and those who of their own rashness assume them to themselves*, are not ministers of the church, but are to be looked upon as thieves and robbers, who have not entered by the door."[13] This is in reference to John 10:1, in which Jesus said, "Truly, truly, I say to you, he who does not enter the sheepfold by the door but climbs in by another way, that man is a thief and a robber" (the "door" here being the legitimate delegation of a shepherd into the sheepfold by the Pope).

Trent is not the only council to have condemned the proposition that the laity could delegate the clergy. The First Lateran Council (1123 AD) stated in Canon 18: "Priests are to be appointed to parish churches by the bishops, to whom they shall answer for the care of souls and for those matters which pertain to the bishop. They may not receive tithes or churches from lay persons without the consent and wish of the bishops; and if they presume to do otherwise, they

---

[12] Marcel Lefebvre, February 20, 1991: *The Archbishop Speaks: Remarks with Respect to the New Bishop*

to Succeed His Excellency Bishop de Castro Mayer, Society of St. Pius X - District of Asia. https://www.sspxasia.com/Documents/Archbishop-Lefebvre/Remarks_New_Bishop_Succeed_Bishop_Mayer.htm

[13] General Council of Trent: Twenty-Third Session, Chapter IV, Papal Encyclicals Online, https://www.papalencyclicals.net/councils/trent/twenty-third-session.htm

shall be subject to the canonical penalty."[14] This canon was then reinforced at the Fourth Lateran Council (1215 AD), which stated, "It was forbidden at the [First] Lateran council, as is known, for any regulars to dare to receive churches or tithes from lay hands without the bishop's consent…We now forbid it even more strongly and will take care to see that offenders are punished with condign penalties."[15] How could this justification be invoked after such repeated and strict condemnations?

This is not only denounced in conciliar texts; the Holy See has likewise denounced it. Pope Bl. Pius IX, ever reliable in his declarations that respond to traditionalist claims, said the following in *Etsi multa* regarding the Old Catholics: "And surely what these sons of perdition intend is quite clear from their other writings… For these writings attack and pervert the true power of jurisdiction of the Roman Pontiff and the bishops, who are the successors of blessed Peter and the apostles; they transfer it instead to the people, or, as they say, to the community."[16] The parallels, once again, are striking, and any support for the traditionalist claims is nullified.

This would represent a complete inversion of the order of the Church, if the people could send the pastors. As Jesus says in John 13:16, "Truly, truly, I say to you, a servant is not greater than his

---

[14] First Lateran Council 1123 A.D, Canon 18, Papal Encyclicals Online, https://www.papalencyclicals.net/councils/ecum09.htm

[15] Fourth Lateran Council : 1215, Constitution 61, Papal Encyclicals Online, https://www.papalencyclicals.net/councils/ecum12-2.htm

[16] Pius IX, *Etsi multa.*

master; *nor is he who is sent greater than he who sent him.*" An inferior cannot delegate a superior to his post. This is simply not how the Church operates.

St. Francis de Sales once again offers some very applicable commentary on this.

> If then they have been sent by the laity, they are not sent in Apostolic fashion, nor legitimately, and their mission is null. In fact, the laity have no mission, and how then shall they give it? How shall they communicate the authority which they have not? And therefore St. Paul, speaking of the priesthood and pastoral order, says: Neither doth any man take the honour to himself but he that is called by God, as Aaron was (Heb. x. 4). [...] Whoever then would assert his mission must not assert it as being from the people nor from secular princes. For Aaron was not called in that way, and we cannot be called otherwise than he was. Finally, that which is less is blessed by the better, as St. Paul says (Heb. vii. 7). The people then cannot send the pastors; for the pastors are greater than the people, and mission is not given without blessing. [...] I omit the disorder which would arise if the people sent; for they could not send to one another, one people having no authority over the other; —and what free play would this give to all sorts of heresies and fancies? It is necessary then that the sheep should receive the shepherd from elsewhere, and should not give him to themselves.[17]

---

[17] Sales, *The Catholic Controversy*, 6.

Abbé Emmanuel Berger, a former priest of the SSPX, wrote the following in 1994 after he left the Society:

> On the problem of mission and the question of our jurisdiction. [...] The thesis accepted as authoritative in the Society is Bishop Tissier's, expressed in his Paris conference of March 1991: on the one hand, he rests his argument on the case of necessity; on the other hand, on the needs of the faithful who turn to us. It is a supplied jurisdiction, or in the end, it is the faithful's request which gives us jurisdiction, case by case. [...] I find it difficult to reconcile this position with the hierarchical structure of the Church, where the apostolate is necessarily based on the mission which can only come from above. It has been written that I have deserted my post and abandoned the flock. But, on the one hand, it was not "my" flock; it had been entrusted to me by superiors to whom this flock did not belong.[18]

The preceding quotes should make it clear. One must be sent, or have a mission; one does not take the responsibility onto themselves. The traditionalists admit they have no ordinary canonical mission, yet they claim to minister on behalf of the Church regardless. This is a precarious situation. "For in effect, to stand up as preacher of God's Word and pastor of souls—what is it but to call oneself ambassador and legate of Our Lord, according to that of the Apostle:

---

[18] Berger, letter to Bishop Bernard Fellay.

We are therefore ambassadors for Christ?"[19] If one purports to be an ambassador for the Lord, yet the Church has not sent him, this is illicitly seizing an office and a power that is exclusive by divine law.

The only remaining appeal that the Church might consider legitimate is what is known as "extraordinary mission," or mission given directly by God instead of through His Church, as has occurred with saintly figures in the Church's past. This stands to reason; if one is not authorized by the Church or by God, they possess no legitimate mission at all, and are simply acting of their own accord.

The traditionalists certainly seem to believe their mission is authorized by God. Take, for example, Archbishop Lefebvre's words, from his letter requesting that his four future bishops accept the episcopacy. He claimed that "God raised up the Priestly Society of St. Pius X for the maintenance and perpetuity of His glorious and expiatory Sacrifice within the Church," that he finds himself "constrained by Divine Providence to pass on the grace of the Catholic episcopacy," and that he is convinced he is "only carrying out the holy will of Our Lord."[20] (Notably, this is also the letter wherein he says that the See of Peter is "occupied by anti-Christs" and that "the destruction of the Kingdom of Our Lord is being rapidly carried out...through the corruption of the Holy Mass," leading to "the universal decadence of Faith[.]")

But there is one factor absolutely necessary to extraordinary mission that the traditionalists lack, and that is miracles.

---

[19] Sales, *The Catholic Controversy*, 3 (emphasis in original)

[20] "Letter to the Future Bishops," SSPX website. https://fsspx.org/en/letter-future-bishops-31130

Why did Jesus work miracles during His public ministry? He himself provides the answer: "But the testimony which I have is greater than that of John; for the works which the Father has granted me to accomplish, these very works which I am doing, bear me witness that the Father has sent me" (Jn 5:36). He further says, "If I am not doing the works of my Father, then do not believe me; but if I do them, even though you do not believe me, believe the works, that you may know and understand that the Father is in me and I am in the Father" (Jn 10:38). He also says, "If I had not done among them the works which no one else did, they would not have sin" (Jn 15:24), to again give authority to His miracles, and to declare that those people would be blameless who would not believe Him if He did not work miracles.

Our Lord's meaning is unmistakable here. Miracles are proof of God's sanction on a certain action or proclamation. As Fulton Sheen wrote, "[Jesus'] miracles were seals which God set upon His revelation of Christ as His divine Son. If Jesus shows it is by His own power He works a miracle, He proves Himself to be Lord of the universe and to be God."[21] Our Lord Himself has established the standard. If one claims to have a mission directly given by God, how are we to know whether this claim is true? By miracles. By seeing that God confirms the testimony that this person brings. The Scriptures give written proof of this besides Jesus' words. As Matthew 9:6-7 says, "But that you may know that the Son of man has authority on earth to forgive sins"—he then said to the paralytic—'Rise, take up your bed and go home.' And he rose and went home." Jesus not only tells

---

[21] Fulton Sheen, *Your Life Is Worth Living* (Schnecksville; St. Andrew's Press, 2014), 42.

us about His power, but He also demonstrates it so that we will know He speaks the truth.

Now it is obvious that Jesus has divine power and can work miracles, so perhaps the case loses some of its weight? Perhaps it is unreasonable to hold mere humans to the same standard? Not so at all. St. Francis de Sales writes, "[N]o one should allege an extraordinary mission unless he prove it by miracles: for, I pray you, where should we be if this pretext of extraordinary mission was to be accepted without proof? [...] Never was any one extraordinarily sent unless he brought this letter of credit from the divine Majesty."[22]

When sent by God to free the Israelites, Moses expressed his hesitation and said, "But behold, they will not believe me or listen to my voice, for they will say, 'The Lord did not appear to you.'" (Ex 4:1) And God grants him the power to work miracles "that they may believe that the Lord, the God of their fathers, the God of Abraham, the God of Isaac, and the God of Jacob, has appeared to you" (Ex 4:5). And when "the Lord said to Moses, "I am the Lord; tell Pharaoh king of Egypt all that I say to you" (Ex 6:29), he knows to grant Moses miraculous power for "[w]hen Pharaoh says to you, '*Prove yourselves by working a miracle*'" (Ex 7:8).

If Moses, a prefigurement of Jesus, required this proof, and if Jesus himself fulfilled that type, how can any future ministers exempt themselves from it? If no miracles accompanied the claim to minister directly on God's behalf, might not anyone seize the opportunity to claim that they were sent by God? Would not chaos erupt when the faithful did not know to whom they should give their obedience?

---

[22] Sales, *The Catholic Controversy*, 9.

As was written in *United States Catholic Magazine*, "It is the duty of him who calls himself an apostle or envoy of heaven, and wishes to be acknowledged as such, to exhibit the authentic proofs and credentials of his commission. If, in order to be invested with apostolic powers, it were enough to claim them and to give one's own bare word for it, every daring innovator would have reason on his side[.]"[23]

Pope Innocent III wrote in *Cum ex injuncto*, "[I]t does not suffice for anyone to assert so boldly that he is sent by God, since any heretic may profess this: but it is necessary that he proves that invisible mission by the working of miracles or by special testimony of the Scriptures. [...] Therefore he who says that he is sent by God should not be believed, since he has not been sent by man, unless he personally offers special testimony from Scripture, or he shows an obvious miracle."[24] St. Francis de Sales, with characteristic bluntness, wrote, "He then who would be so rash as to boast of extraordinary mission without immediately producing miracles, deserves to be taken for an impostor."[25]

With this precedent affirmed by Our Lord himself, in His own words, let us apply it to the context of the traditionalists. Where are their miracles? What proof can they present of a divine commission, since they have no commission from the Church? Why should we

---

[23] I. Daniel Rupp, *Apostolicity of the Church*, United States Catholic Magazine, December 1844. https://books.google.com/books?id=MkA9-AAAAYAAJ&pg=PA757), 758.

[24] Innocent III, *Cum ex injuncto* (1199). https://en.wikisource.org/wiki/Translation:Cum_ex_injuncto

[25] Sales, *The Catholic Controversy*, 10.

believe them and follow them, if this is the standard set by the Church and they have failed to produce any "letters of credit?"

Abbé Emmanuel Berger conceded to this precedent and recognized that miracles were indeed necessary to prove it. He wrote that he asked Bishop Tissier de Mallerais for a defense of the illicit consecrations of 1988, to which Bishop de Mallerais cited, among other reasons, "divine inspiration given to the Archbishop (Lefebvre)." Berger responded that "if there has been divine inspiration or an exception willed by God, it is subject to the same rules as any apparition or charism and must be authenticated by the Church's legitimate authority; in any case, we are entitled to have some public and unquestionable public sign. Failing which, we can but hold to the general law of the Church."[26]

As stated, mission is essential for an ecclesiastical ministry, and can only be given by the Church or by God himself. Yet the traditionalists have not received a mission from either one. Their bishops have no jurisdiction over any priest or any flock, yet they send priests to minister to sheepfolds over which they have not been authorized by the supreme authority. This is directly contradictory to the nature of mission in the Church. Jesus says in the Gospel of John, "He who speaks on his own authority seeks his own glory; but he who seeks the glory of him who sent him is true, and in him there is no falsehood" (Jn 7:18). The traditionalist position fails in all respects to meet the necessary requirements for a legitimate mission, without which one cannot claim the privilege of ministering in the name of Christ.

---

[26] Berger, letter to Bishop Bernard Fellay.

5.

The State of Necessity

We have established that a lawful mission is necessary to minister on behalf of Christ's Church. Having no ordinary canonical mission, and unable to demonstrate miraculous proof of an extraordinary mission, the traditionalists have no legitimate mission to speak of. Nonetheless, they posit that a state of necessity, created by the crisis situation in the Church today, authorizes their ministry. Assuming for the sake of the argument that there is somehow a defense for a ministry which has not been lawfully delegated nor divinely authorized, let us proceed with examining their reasoning.

The Holy See has in fact explicitly condemned the idea that an appeal to necessity can be invoked for a mission contrary to the lawful mission of the Church. Over two hundred years ago, in 1791, Pope Pius VI issued his encyclical *Charitas*, responding to the errors of the Civil Constitution of the Clergy during the French Revolution. Referring to several priests who were illicitly consecrated bishops in the same manner as traditionalist bishops, i.e., by bishops who did not possess any jurisdiction nor the required mandate from the Holy See, Pius VI made clear their lack of canonical mission and the erroneous defense they claimed to substitute for it.

We similarly declare and decree that their consecrations were sinful, and are illicit, unlawful, sacrilegious, and at variance with the regulations of the sacred canons; since they were rashly and wrongfully elected, they lack all ecclesiastical and spiritual jurisdiction for the guidance of souls, and have been suspended from all exercise of the episcopal office. [...] We therefore severely forbid the…wickedly elected and illicitly consecrated men, under this punishment of suspension, to assume episcopal jurisdiction or any other authority for the guidance of souls since they have never received it. *Nor must they appoint, depute, or confirm pastors, vicars, missionaries, helpers, functionaries, ministers, or others, whatever their title, for the care of souls and the administration of the Sacraments under any pretext of necessity whatsoever.*[1]

The argument for a state of necessity holds no weight after such an explicit condemnation as this, when the context is identical and the same defense is identified.

Another less explicit but still applicable historical example is the schismatic Armenians of Constantinople in the late 19th century, of whom Bl. Pope Pius IX wrote, "They have claimed also that they are unable to accept the sentence [of schism and excommunication] because the faithful might desert to the heretics if deprived of their ministration. These novel arguments were wholly unknown and unheard of by the ancient Fathers of the Church."[2] If the Armenians, who believed their ministry was necessary to avert what they perceived as true heresy, could not legitimately invoke a "state of necessity," how much less could those who likewise invoke it to combat

---

[1] Pius VI, *Charitas* (1791), Papal Encyclicals Online, https://www.papalencyclicals.net/pius06/p6charit.htm

[2] Pius IX, *Quartus supra.*

mere "ambiguities" or "confusion?" Why could a state of necessity be invoked for a lesser offense and be justifiable?

The Holy See is not the only source to have denounced the "state of necessity" defense. We also find this in the writings of Rev. John MacHale, who addressed the state of necessity in 1842:

> [T]hose who, in every age, have obtruded themselves into the sanctuary without any authentic evidence of their delegation, have been treated as usurpers. [...] *In vain will such arrogant individuals plead the corruption of the Church of Christ, to colour with the plea of necessity their own usurpation.* [...] If, therefore, any are deluded by the specious invectives of the sectaries against the corruption of the apostolical ministry, they must be the willing dupes of error; since the divine commission of our Redeemer which he has never yet recalled, is a standing pledge of its indefectibility.[3]

Rev. MacHale's statement introduces a crucial connection. If the entire Church has fallen so far into corruption that invoking a state of necessity is the only way to salvage the wreckage of the Barque, this would mean the Church has failed to do what she was established to do; namely, lead souls to heaven. Traditionalists hold that the entire Church is compromised, even where other licit communities like the FSSP have a presence. If the Church has failed in her mission and requires vagus priests to minister against her shepherds, the gates of hell have certainly prevailed, something we have

---

[3] John MacHale, *The Evidences and Doctrines of the Catholic Church.* (London: Dolman, 1842) 350-351.

assurance from Christ Himself will never happen. Ex-SSPX priest Gary Cambell wrote the following in 1999, in his letter explaining why he was leaving the Society: "Despite our laboured attempts to theologically explain things away, we must state that the Church has erred: that is, it has failed to lead souls to heaven. [...] Despite our earnest protests to the contrary, we cannot avoid practical heresy in asserting that the Church is not indefectible."[4]

If their ministry is necessary because the Church is *not* providing for the salvation of souls, how does one admit she has not defected? And if she has not defected, why is their ministry necessary? Do individual bishops who lack authority over any dioceses, and "wandering" priests who lack any ordinary canonical mission, presume to possess something necessary for salvation that "the church of the living God, the pillar and bulwark of the truth" (1 Tim 3:15) does not? To again cite St. Francis de Sales, "[T]o be a pillar of truth cannot appertain to an erring and straying Church."[5]

An article in *United States Catholic Magazine* addressed this very question in 1844 and is worth quoting at length here.

> [The Protestants] maintain that a stern necessity, occasioned by the wretched and corrupt state of the Roman church at the time of the reformation, obliged them to set up a new ministry. [...] This too was the plea alleged by the Arians, the

---

[4] Fr. Gary Campbell to Bishop Bernard Fellay, May 4, 1999, *Why Do Priests Leave the SSPX?* https://www.tapatalk.com/groups/ignis_ardens/viewtopic.php?f=11&t=11560&sid=7bde6-64ef4a544b05fb9a1924a-9c57db&view=print

[5] Sales, *The Catholic Controversy*, 41.

Manicheans, and other sectarians of ancient times, in support of their attempt to remodel the church[.] [...] Can it be
said, will it be said that all these were in the right? Assuredly
not; yet they did at one time merely what the reformers did
some centuries later; they proceeded in the same way, and
gave the same proofs of their mission, that is to say, their own
assertion, their bold invectives, and a presumptuous declaration they were more enlightened and understood the doctrines of Christianity better than the Christian church itself.

Necessity of setting up a new ministry! But where is it
written in the authentic records of divine revelation, that necessity can found a divine mission? We read in the Scripture:
"Neither doth any man take the honor to himself, but he that
is called by God, as Aaron was." Where do we read "neither
doth any man take the honor to himself, but he that is called
to it by necessity?" We learn also from St. Paul that "no one
can preach, unless he be sent." But where is it said, "except
in the case of necessity?" Necessity, therefore, is in this case
an unmeaning word. [...] What becomes, in this supposi-
tion, of our Lord's unconditional promises, according to
which the gates of hell shall never prevail *against it*, and he
himself will be with its pastors all days even to the consum-
mation of the world?[6]

As we can see, the "state of necessity" defense has been invoked
before, and for more serious reasons than what the traditionalists

---

[6] Rupp, *Apostolicity of the Church*, 766-767 (emphasis in original)

claim. It was not satisfactory to the Church then, and it therefore cannot be now. Ex-SSPX priest Marshall Roberts said the following in 1997: "We in the Society of St. Pius X always argued a case of necessity, but Rome has answered the argument: such a case could not exist, for it would imply that there was a deficiency in God's providence over the Church. To save the Church, one should have to bypass the papacy, which is the source of all the Church's unity."[7]

An Old Testament parallel may be of use here. In Genesis, God promised Abram that he would be the father of innumerable descendants. We read that Abram "believed the LORD, and he reckoned it to him as righteousness" (Gen 15:6) but his wife Sar'ai did not. Being barren, she convinced Abram to conceive a child with her maidservant Hagar, saying, "Behold now, the LORD has prevented me from bearing children; go in to my maid; it may be that I shall obtain children by her" (Gen 16:2). She did not trust that the Lord's covenant could be fulfilled, as all natural circumstances seemed to indicate that it could not, so she and Abram took it upon themselves to attempt to fulfill this covenant through illicit means.

Did Abram and his wife not also see a necessity to take matters into their own hands? God himself came down and passed between the pieces of the animals Abram had offered for the covenant; there is no doubt as to its veracity. Yet they doubted, and felt they had to fulfill it by their own efforts. They lost their faith and trust in God when it seemed there was no other way. Likewise, Jesus gave His

---

[7] Fr. Marshall Roberts, December 8, 1997, *Why Do Priests Leave the SSPX?* https://www.tapatalk.com/groups/ignis_ardens/viewtopic.php?f=11&t=11560&sid=7bde664ef4a544b05fb9a-1924a9c57db&view=print

own self in the Eucharist for the New Covenant, an "eternal" covenant, one that was entrusted to the apostles and was promised to last
forever. Yet some successors of the apostles, such as Archbishop
Lefebvre and other independent bishops, doubted that this covenant
could still be fulfilled when certain circumstances were introduced,
i.e., a new rite of ordination or Mass that they believed may not be
valid and could lead to the Church's long, slow death. Archbishop
Lefebvre said that it would be impossible for seminarians to approach "conciliar bishops, who, due to their doubtful intentions,
confer doubtful sacraments," and that "what we have been doing is
just what is necessary for the reconstruction of the Church."[8] Clergy
members such as Lefebvre took it upon themselves to ensure that
the means for maintaining the existence of the Church (valid bishops and priests) were available, regardless of whether this conflicted
with Christ's promise of indefectibility or whether it was licit to do
so. They similarly lost their faith and trust in the Church.

By establishing a worldwide ministry, the traditionalists cannot
escape the conclusion that they believe the Church has defected.
They demonstrate by their own actions that nowhere is orthodoxy
maintained, nowhere does a lawful prelate hold authority to which
a priest must be subject, and nowhere is the crisis abated to such a
degree that they are not needed. Fr. Ramon Angles of the SSPX states
the traditionalist position very clearly: "The faithful who have recourse to a Modernist priest put their very faith in danger of compromising with the post-conciliar Liberal doctrines...perpetrated in

---

[8] Marcel Lefebvre, "1988 Episcopal Consecrations sermon," SSPX
website.   https://sspx.org/en/1988-episcopal-consecrations-sermon-of-
archbishop-lefebvre

virtually every 'modern' parish in the world. ...[T]hey cannot have recourse to any authorized priest without putting their soul in grave danger of compromising, diminishing or even losing their faith."[9] How can one say this and still profess that the gates of hell have not prevailed against the Church? It is an absolute contradiction, and one that no Catholic can support.

To again cite St. Francis de Sales:

> How, I ask you, should he have abandoned the Church, which cost him all his blood, so many toils and travails? He has drawn Israel out of Egypt, out of the desert, out of the Red Sea, out of so many calamities and captivities and we are to believe that he has let Christianity be engulfed in infidelity! [...] Oh, how utterly vain and good for nothing would be the promises on promises which he has made of the perpetuity of this Church![10]

There is no situation so dire that it would demand that priests and bishops minister against the established order of the entire Church. The reasons that would justify such a ministry are simply irreconcilable with Catholic dogma and would imply that Our Lord deceived us when He said, "I am with you always, to the close of the age" (Matt 28:20). Yet again, the support for the traditionalist position shows itself to be indefensible.

---

[9] Ramon Angles, "Validity of SSPX's confessions & marriages (2)." https://sspx.org/en/validity-sspxs-confessions-marriages-2

[10] Sales, *The Catholic Controversy*, 35

6.

Supplied Jurisdiction

With the exception of the SSPX, whose priests currently possess a particularly unique form of jurisdiction from Pope Francis for absolving sins and can witness marriages in dioceses where the local bishop has permitted them, no traditionalist group has any delegated jurisdiction from the lawful diocesan bishop or the Holy See. As such, they rely on the concept of "supplied jurisdiction" to operate. I have shown in the previous chapter how no state of necessity can generate such a form of jurisdiction, but it merits examination, nonetheless.

Firstly, allow me to present the rationale for traditionalist supplied jurisdiction, given to us by the SSPX:

The current crisis in the Church has created a state of necessity which justifies and requires traditional priests to fulfill their duties even without having ordinary jurisdiction (that is, having faculties to exercise a priestly ministry). Every member of the Church has the right to receive the doctrine and sacraments necessary for salvation. This right is embodied in the Code of Canon Law which declares that the supreme law is the salvation of souls. So, if the hierarchy (pastor, bishop, etc.) does not fulfill its duty, the faithful find themselves in a state of necessity which allows them to have recourse to any Catholic priest. In consequence of this state of necessity, such a priest receives directly from the Church what is called supplied jurisdiction in order to minister to the faithful.[1]

The Church does indeed supply jurisdiction to priests who do not have it, in certain circumstances; namely, when there is danger of death, common error, or positive and probable doubt, per canons 144 and 976 of the 1983 Code of Canon Law (canons 209 and 882 of the 1917 Code). Obviously, the danger of death does not provide the faculty for everyday ministry. Common error and positive or probable doubt are based on if the people are genuinely mistaken as to whether the priest possesses faculties delegated by the local bishop, or if the priest is unsure of whether his faculty is present or has expired. Neither seems to apply, as both the traditionalist priests and faithful who follow them are quite aware that the local bishop has not authorized their ministry. How, then, do they leverage this to their advantage?

While the sacraments they administer in danger of death are indeed legitimate, as the Church permits any priest (even an excommunicated one) to hear confessions in danger of death, how do the other two criteria apply? Fr. Ramon Angles of the SSPX attempts to provide an explanation, which strangely concludes with the rationale that to "induce the error" in a community is enough to provide the faculty. As he states, "[E]ven though nobody in the community is mistaken about the lack of jurisdiction...[if] a public fact is repeatedly presented which by its nature may induce the faithful to

---

[1] "Do priests of the SSPX have jurisdiction?" SSPX Website. https://sspx.org/en/do-priests-of-the-sspx-have-jurisdiction-sspx-faq-ep13-resource

believe that the priest has the faculties, …[t]he mere FACT that we administer habitually the Sacraments to some community of faithful is sufficient to apply the doctrine of common error."[2] This is an odd conclusion; it certainly sounds like he is saying that all a priest needs to do is deceive the faithful into thinking he has the faculty by administering a sacrament enough times to "induce" them to error, and the Church will then provide said faculty. If they know he does not have delegated jurisdiction, will continuing to do it somehow convince them?

I am not a canonist, and so I will not attempt to refute his (very extensive) presentation here. However, there are several practical considerations that I think weaken, if not remove, the support on which this argument sits, in the context of the traditionalist ministry.

The most glaring inconsistency with supplied jurisdiction is the circumstances of its application. If the Church is in such a state of emergency that the proper delegation for sacraments is not needed, couldn't any priest in the world operate under supplied jurisdiction? Exercising priestly functions without any limitations is quite the golden ticket, yet it seems only the traditionalists have had the intellectual clarity to take advantage of this. Can a diocesan priest or FSSP priest publicly witness marriages or offer Mass in another diocese without the bishop's approval? If not, why not? Isn't there a state of necessity? Aren't his services needed?

[2] Ramon Angles, "Validity of SSPX's confessions & marriages," SSPX Website. https://sspx.org/en/validity-sspxs-confessions-marriages

It certainly seems that the canonical logic that traditionalists rely on supports this theory. Fr. Ramon Angles' study of supplied jurisdiction cited previously also says that, based on the canonical implications of common error, "[I]f a priest without jurisdiction to hear confessions sits in a confessional or puts on a purple stole indicating that he is ready to hear confessions, the Church will supply his lack of jurisdiction for every absolution he will give."[3] (The article reassures readers that this is "sound canonical doctrine.") But this does not make sense. If sacraments could be celebrated wherever and whenever a priest chose, no priest would ever be liable for unlawful use of faculties; a casual appeal to "supplied jurisdiction" would exempt him from any disciplinary action by his bishop.

Or does this unique situation of supplied jurisdiction only apply to the traditionalists? If so, when may a priest invoke this "supplied jurisdiction" if he left his diocese and joined them? Traditionalist groups are not granting this jurisdiction; it is not even a form that can be granted. They simply assume it onto themselves, transforming it from an exception to a rule, and rely on it for the entirety of their ministry. If this jurisdiction is something only they can claim, a newly recruited priest clearly did not have it at one point (and was subject to the authority granted by his bishop), but then upon joining them, he somehow obtained it, and apparently is no longer subject to the authority of that same bishop. What has changed? Nothing, except his interior disposition and intentions. And if he were to leave them and return to his bishop, when and how would he lose the ability to invoke it? Is it just by some vague, nebulous adherence

---

[3] Ibid.

to their theological stance? Is it by his willingness to submit to an authority or not? Again, there is no clear answer. This would indicate an unsettling instability and weakness in the Church, if jurisdiction to administer sacraments was based on such subjective grounds.

This presents two possibilities. On the one hand, if every priest in the world can legitimately invoke supplied jurisdiction at any time and in any place (seeing as how the crisis affects the entire Church), it essentially denies the authority of every bishop worldwide, and reduces a diocese from the sheepfold of an apostle's successor to nothing more than a legal entity existing for tax purposes. At that point, a bishop's only role would be to function as an administrator for a geographic area, without holding any governing power over the priests under his authority. This is simply contrary to the very nature of the episcopal office. As Pope Leo XIII wrote in his encyclical *Satis cognitum* regarding the office and power of the bishop, "It is not sufficient for the due preservation of the unity of the faith that the head should merely have been charged with the office of superintendent, or should have been invested solely with a power of direction. But it is absolutely necessary that he should have received real and sovereign authority which the whole community is bound to obey."[4]

On the other hand, if only traditionalist priests can claim this form of jurisdiction, it becomes valid or invalid for priests joining

---

[4] Leo XIII, *Satis cognitum* (1896), Papal Encyclicals Online, https://www.papalencyclicals.net/leo13/l13satis.htm

and leaving them...somehow, in a way that does not seem to be objectively verifiable. If we cannot define when and how it is gained and lost, how can the laity know whether a priest even possesses it at all? Is it dispensed solely based on the personal intention of administering sacraments to combat the crisis? Jurisdiction is not a personal, individual power that can be enabled and disabled on a whim. It is either delegated by a lawful authority, or supplied by the Church as circumstances demand. Were the circumstances absent when this priest was serving in his diocese, then suddenly present when he joined a traditionalist group? As stated, no bishop or group can grant supplied jurisdiction, so in this hypothetical scenario, it seems as though it "activates" based on a priest's subjective, internal acquiescence to the existence of the necessity, and could "deactivate" just as quickly if he denied that the necessity was there. This makes no more sense than the alternative.

Surely the traditionalists have the honesty to admit that there is no historical, traditional, or canonical precedent for obtaining universal jurisdiction based on personal intention. One might take their accusation that "Novus Ordo sacraments" are of dubious validity based on the priest's intention, or potential lack thereof, and apply it back to them in the case of jurisdiction. If jurisdiction is received based on intention, how are we to know whether their intention is there? Would this not be grounds for just as legitimate a doubt about the liceity, and in some cases, validity, of their sacraments, as they have about "Novus Ordo sacraments?" If jurisdiction is required for sacraments, as they would concede, but we do not know when or how a traditionalist priest has obtained this unique form of jurisdiction that no other priest can claim, could any lay person ever be convinced that their sacraments were actually legitimate?

The idea that only traditionalist priests can take advantage of this supplied jurisdiction, then, seems to be indefensible. It must be universal. Their defenses for it certainly seem to confirm that, as Fr. Angles' canonical study says that if a priest *without jurisdiction* publicly indicates he is ready to hear confession, the Church will supply the faculty. A priest from one diocese who goes over to another without permission does not have jurisdiction there, but apparently the Church will simply grant it if he dons a purple stole and sits in a confessional. So, by their own logic, any priest can hear confessions anywhere he likes, and he will always have the faculty, which naturally would then extend to the administration of all other sacraments.

How could this possibly be conducive to the proper order of the Church? If this is something the Church permitted in her law, why did she never concede that previous dissenters were correct? Why were no schismatics or sectarians of past centuries justified in their actions, when this was a valid defense and available to them? Supplied jurisdiction was not suddenly invented when canon law was codified; it is a principle that already existed in the Church. Did none of them think to invoke it? What missteps did they take that the traditionalists have so carefully avoided?

Not only would universal supplied jurisdiction nullify apostolic authority, but it also negates the concept of jurisdiction entirely. In practice, traditionalists equate Holy Orders with jurisdiction, because once they are ordained, they minister wherever and whenever they please, and require no legitimate delegation to any particular geographic area. Their priests may minister in one diocese just as easily as another; there are no hindrances.

The supplied jurisdiction they claim to have is, for all intents and purposes, not any form of jurisdiction at all. They erase the necessary distinction between the "can" of Holy Orders and the "may" of jurisdiction. All they have, and all they need, is "can." Where may they *not* go? What sacraments may they *not* administer? The answer, of course, is "nowhere" and "none." Jurisdiction means nothing here because there is no circumstance in which they do *not* have jurisdiction. If a doctor could practice medicine anywhere in the world, what would be the point of a medical license? Why even have one? It means nothing; all he really needs to demonstrate his qualification is his diploma.

The inevitable traditionalist rebuttal to this is that the entire Church is in the equivalent of a disaster scenario, where medical licenses indeed mean nothing; people just need medical care. But this again implies that Christ would allow the Church to lose all form of governance and be plunged into chaos, without any sort of guidance or leadership, and where everyone must fend for themselves and request the sacraments from anyone who can provide them. This is simply incompatible with the dogma of indefectibility. Can Christ's promise of "I am with you always" be true if no leadership and no order is left in the Church? The SSPX states that this defense may be invoked "if the hierarchy (pastor, bishop, etc.) does not fulfill its duty": does this mean to imply that no priest or bishop anywhere in the world is fulfilling his duty? That is quite a serious charge.

Another issue with supplied jurisdiction is its function. The circumstances which supply jurisdiction for priests are centered around the administration of sacraments. They do not in any way apply to building churches, establishing schools and seminaries, issuing dispensations from vows, or any of the other public activities associated with the traditionalist movement. How could the danger of death or error of a community as to whether the priest has a faculty be applied in the case of building a church, for example?

If traditionalist priests functioned within its actual limits, they would essentially have to administer sacraments when requested by the faithful on a case-by-case basis, and become a kind of "priest for rent," without assuming residence in a chapel or establishing their own communities. Yet invoking supplied jurisdiction is the justification for all their ministerial activities. The SSPX even invoked it to "supply" a papal mandate for their episcopal consecrations (with the explanation that "the 'Roman Church' of 19 centuries (excluding Vatican II) 'orders' those who have remained faithful to the Magisterium to 'faithfully transmit' the Deposit of the Faith for the salvation of souls"),[5] and for erecting its tribunal that issues declarations of marriage nullity which are not recognized by the Church. (Applicants to their tribunal are required to swear on the Bible that they will not approach the lawful diocesan tribunal![6])

---

[5] "A canonical study of the 1988 consecrations (3)," SSPX Website. https://sspx.org/en/canonical-study-1988-consecrations-3

[6] "An approach to declarations of nullity," SSPX Website. https://sspx.org/en/approach-declarations-nullity. The existence of this tribunal has caused a number of priests to leave the SSPX when they realized it was nothing less than a competing authority to the Church, despite

A final consideration is this. All traditionalist groups operate under the "state of necessity" justification, and so their supplied jurisdiction they claim to have is bound to the existence of the crisis. This is confirmed in the words of the SSPX: "This grave situation has led to a state of necessity, which is the basis for the supplied jurisdiction that applies to the SSPX's priests in exercising their ministry for the salvation of souls."[7]

The reason supplied jurisdiction is most often associated with danger of death is because that is an objectively verifiable fact. If someone is bleeding out on the side of the road, jurisdiction is supplied for the sacraments, and nobody would argue that. But when traditionalists are the ones defining the state of necessity, they would also have to define when and how it ends. Would that not allow them to move the goalposts as they please in order to retain the supplied jurisdiction they claim to have? In one hundred years or so, when the Church is flourishing (and this will certainly happen, if we follow the trajectory of previous councils and their aftermaths), will they still be appealing to a state of necessity? They cannot do this forever.

The crisis must end at some point. But after establishing chapels, schools, seminaries, and communities around the world, and with the SSPX crowning their organization with a multi-million dollar "Mass center" (as they call them) in St. Marys, Kansas, will they be willing to give all that up? Will they be willing to one day admit the

---

the SSPX repeatedly stating they never intended to create a parallel structure.

[7] "Responding to false accusations," SSPX Website. https://sspx.org/en/responding-to-false-accusations

state of necessity is over, thereby removing any reason to appeal to supplied jurisdiction? Will the crisis ever truly end?

One need not investigate canonical subtleties to see how this is problematic. Traditionalists have spilled much ink to ensure their stance aligns with ecclesiastical precedent, but simple logic shows its inconsistency. Either jurisdiction is contingent on personal intention and can be gained or lost depending on one's acknowledgement of an ideology, or the Church has effectively lost her mark of apostolicity, and her authority is no more than some sort of spiritual placebo effect. Neither of these options is defensible in light of Catholic tradition, which reveals the faulty premise on which their ministry is based.

PART III

TRADITIONALISM
AND THE CHURCH

7.

Apostolic Authority

As I have demonstrated regarding the traditionalists' supplied jurisdiction they claim, the evidence seems to be more in favor of the proposition that it is universally applicable and can be claimed by any priest. Traditionalists would likely deny that diocesan priests could operate under supplied jurisdiction, but then the burden is on them to explain why and how this jurisdiction only applies to them. Their words and actions certainly imply that any priest in the world could invoke it. No traditionalist group considers itself subject to any lawful bishop, and Fr. Ramon Angles of the SSPX admits that traditionalist priests carry out all the functions of a public ministry "without the delegation of the diocesan prelate and often very much against his will."[1] Fr. Jonathan Loop concedes in Episode 44 of their Crisis podcast series that they operate "contrary to the known intentions, the known will, of those successors of the Apostles, the Princes of the Church."[2] They establish chapels, schools, seminaries, and religious houses all without the permission of the local bishop, and in fact continue to operate even when the bishop has denied them his blessing to do so (as Fr. Loop admits in the same episode).

---

[1] Ramon Angles, "Validity of SSPX's confessions & marriages," SSPX Website. https://sspx.org/en/validity-sspxs-confessions-marriages

[2] SSPX New - English, "Crisis Series #44: How Can the SSPX Justify What it Does?" YouTube, October 8, 2021, 6:12, https://youtube.com/watch?v=pUvMW_WzJRs

I commend them for their honesty, but it must be stated une-quivocally—there is simply no justification in Catholic tradition for a worldwide, public ministry exercised in direct opposition to the Church's lawful bishops. This is impossible. All precedent explicitly condemns this, beginning at the Church's inception when Christ said to the apostles (and therefore to their successors), "He who hears you hears me, and he who rejects you rejects me" (Lk 10:16). How can one be following the order established by Jesus himself if they reject the authority of every single one of the apostles' successors? As stated before, if a priest or bishop could decide for them-selves where and when to minister, based on their own private judg-ment, what weight does the episcopal character and the power of the hierarchy hold? Why even have bishops at all?

As Pope Gregory XVI wrote in his encyclical *Mirari vos* (a favor-ite amongst traditionalists for its condemnations of religious indif-ferentism):

> Nor may the priests ever forget that they are forbidden by ancient canons to undertake ministry and to assume the tasks of teaching and preaching "without the permission of their bishop to whom the people have been entrusted; an ac-counting for the souls of the people will be demanded from the bishop." *Finally let them understand that all those who struggle against this established order disturb the position of the Church.*[3]

---

[3] Gregory XVI, *Mirari vos* (1832), Papal Encyclicals Online, https://www.papalencyclicals.net/greg16/g16mirar.htm

This "established order" is imperative for maintaining unity in the Church. As early as the second century, St. Ignatius of Antioch was instructing the Church to "obey the bishop and the presbytery with an undivided mind, breaking one and the same bread,"[4] and commanding them "not to set [y]ourselves in opposition to the bishop, in order that [you] may be subject to God."[5] He even went so far as to say, "He who honours the bishop has been honoured by God; he who does anything without the knowledge of the bishop, does [in reality] serve the devil."[6]

The mark of apostolicity is not merely titular; it carries the power of authority as well. If no bishop held any real authority to which priests and faithful must submit, the Church quite simply does not exist, because its apostolic power to teach, govern, and sanctify would mean nothing. Anyone could do what one thought was best, and there would be no central authority to regulate ecclesiastical discipline. As the Apostolic Constitutions dictated in the earliest centuries of the Church, "As, therefore, it was not lawful for one of another tribe, that was not a Levite, to offer anything, or to approach the altar without the priest, so also do you do nothing without the

---

[4] Ignatius of Antioch, *The Epistle of Ignatius to the Ephesians*, Ch. 20. Retrieved from New Advent, https://www.newadvent.org/fathers/0104.htm

[5] Ibid., Ch. 5.

[6] Ignatius of Antioch, *The Epistle of Ignatius to the Smyrneans*, Ch. 9. Retrieved from New Advent, https://www.newadvent.org/fathers/0109.htm

bishop; for if any one does anything without the bishop, he does it to no purpose. For it will not be esteemed as of any avail to him."[7]

Pope Bl. Pius IX wrote in his encyclical *Quartus supra:* "For the Church consists of the people in union with the priest, and the flock following its shepherd. Consequently the bishop is in the Church and the Church in the bishop, *and whoever is not with the bishop is not in the Church.*"[8] A prominent SSPX spokesman used this quote in a public debate against a sedevacantist,[9] attempting to discredit his position and trap him by asking if there is any bishop in the world to which he is subject. But this spokesman somehow failed to recognize that the organization he follows is guilty of the same thing, as is confirmed by the SSPX priests' statements above.

Ex-SSPX priest Fr. Marshall Roberts said the following regarding this issue:

> It is not enough to have the Faith: one must be subject to one's lawful pastors. Who are these? The Catechism continues, "By 'lawful pastors' we mean those in the Church who have been appointed by lawful authority, and who have therefore a right to rule us. The lawful pastors in the Church are: every priest in his own parish, every bishop in his own

---

[7] Apostolic Constitutions, Book II, Section 4, XXVII. Retrieved from New Advent, https://www.newadvent.org/fathers/07152.htm

[8] Pius IX, *Quartus supra.*

[9] Pints With Aquinas, "Sedevacantism Debate: Are John XXIII Through Francis True Popes? Jeff Cassman Vs Br. Peter Dimond," YouTube, September 20, 2022, 1:39:00, https://www.youtube.com/watch?v=tIauJB2_y1c

diocese, and the Pope in the whole Church." If one is not subject to the lawful pastors, one is not in the Church. [...] There is no question that a person can simply ignore his lawful pastor as if he did not exist.[10]

As shown regarding the importance of mission, the Church must be guided by lawful delegation; otherwise, any bishop or priest could do as he saw fit. The Council of Trent, so often cited by the traditionalists in their defenses, forbade any priestly ministry to be undertaken without the consent of the lawful authority. Session XXIII of Trent stated the following: "Furthermore, no cleric, who is a stranger, shall, without letters commendatory from his own Ordinary, be admitted by any bishop to celebrate the divine mysteries, and to administer the sacraments."[11] This explicitly condemns the actions of traditionalist clergy, all of whom are "strangers" as they are not incardinated into any diocese, and who have no commendatory (i.e., dimissorial) letters from their Ordinary (i.e., bishop), because they do not *have* an Ordinary. Trent also declared that "no one, whether Secular or Regular, shall presume to preach, even in churches of his own order, in opposition to the will of the bishop."[12]

An equally problematic but at least more honest approach would be for them to assess the situation of a specific diocese, decide

---

[10] Roberts, letter.

[11] General Council of Trent: Twenty-Third Session, Decree on Reformation, Chapter XVI, Papal Encyclicals Online, https://www.papalencyclicals.net/councils/trent/twenty-third-session.htm

[12] General Council of Trent: Twenty-Fourth Session, Decree on Reformation, Chapter IV, Papal Encyclicals Online, https://www.papalencyclicals.net/councils/trent/twenty-fourth-session.htm

whether the bishop and his priests are orthodox enough, and then establish a ministry based on that decision. But again, this introduces yet another layer of subjectivity. If the determination is based on individual opinion, what happens if one vagus priest decides a diocese needs his help, but another disagrees? Who is right? What gives one the authority to make this decision over another? Is orthodoxy measured based on one's own criteria?

A further consideration is as follows. The Church's own law can in no way provide for the universal and unrestricted jurisdiction of any priest against her bishops and her priests in communion with each other. That would imply that the Church herself could sanction a ministry against her "essential constitution," as Pope Leo XIII termed it, or that the Church could internally work against herself, as if the Bride could somehow legitimately oppose the Bridegroom. It means canon law is so deficient or so faulty that, despite two thousand years of precedent, the Church could foresee, permit, and even require a ministry that necessarily opposes the government of her shepherds. It means that despite all her previous condemnations of ministering against the will of the bishop, exceptions to that standard do in fact exist, and that when the Church codified her canon law in 1917, she felt the need to ensure a failsafe was in place, as if her apostolic authority and indefectibility needed some kind of insurance besides being guaranteed by Christ Himself. Would this not display a massive lack of trust in the Savior's words?

We also must consider the practical implications of separating from the lawful authority, both that of the bishops and of the pope. To whom do the traditionalists answer, and for what are they accountable? They do not answer to the Pope; their movement is built on rejecting his declarations. They do not answer to the local bishop; they operate in direct opposition to him, by their own admission. And they cannot answer to their own bishops because, frankly, they are not "their" bishops. They are bishops by consecration only and are not any priest's legitimate superior. Do the traditionalists recognize any legitimate authority figure? It seems that the answer is no.

Responding to the question of what they would do if the local bishop approached them and ordered them to cease their ministry in his diocese, Fr. David Sherry of the SSPX claims that an order of this kind would indicate that "the bishop is not in his right mind, because he wants to get rid of what we always had, and what we always had is the faith, and that's why I am justified in not doing that."[13] In their minds, the hierarchy truly is trying to undermine or destroy the faith, and they are the only ones preserving it. See, for example, the declaration of Bishop Michael Sheridan regarding the Servants of the Holy Family, a traditionalist group established in the diocese of Colorado Springs after their founder broke away from the SSPX. Bishop Sheridan declared in no uncertain terms that the group is not in good standing with the Church, that they are forbidden to carry out a public ministry, and that the faithful should avoid them.[14] Similar diocesan statements about other traditionalist communities around the country can be easily found. Yet these groups

---

[13] SSPX News - English, "Why The SSPX Is Correct - SSPX Interview Series—Episode 7," YouTube, March 3, 2023, 1:33:06, https://www.youtube.com/watch?v=zQBRBu6Xu0I

[14] Declaration of The Most Reverend Michael J. Sheridan, S.Th.D., by the Grace of God and the Apostolic See, Bishop of Colorado Springs, July 31, 2013, https://www.diocs.org/Portals/0/Documents/All%20Things%20

continue to operate because the prelate from whom they derived established a precedent with the "state of necessity" and "salvation of souls" excuse, which serves as the justification for every action they take.

The traditionalists also submit to no punishment or reprimand. Archbishop Lefebvre himself said that since Vatican II, the Church has "acted contrary to the Holy Tradition," and as he wrote, "This is why we reckon of no value all the penalties and all the censures inflicted by these authorities."[15] When one group sets this precedent and thereby encourages other groups to do the same, they then have no qualms about opposing the Church and shrugging off her penal declarations. Never have they admitted that any sanction or censure applies to them. Pope St. Pius X said the following about the Modernists in *Pascendi*; does this not apply to the traditionalists just as accurately? "Finally, and this almost destroys all hope of cure, their very doctrines have given such a bent to their minds, that they disdain all authority and brook no restraint; and relying upon a false conscience, they attempt to ascribe to a love of truth that which is in reality the result of pride and obstinacy."[16]

This mode of operating cannot in any way be legitimate in light of true Catholic tradition and history. Regarding those who had "the pretension...to escape the jurisdiction of ecclesiastical authority,"

Catholic/BishopSheridanDecreeOnServantsOfTheHolyFamily.pdf?ver=UPhpHNu2ZR3SVu16NIVG-w%3D%3D

[15] A canonical study of the 1988 consecrations (3)," SSPX Website. https://sspx.org/en/canonical-study-1988-consecrations-3

[16] Pius X, *Pascendi dominici gregis.*

the traditionalist champion Pope St. Pius X wrote, "Even if their doctrines were free from errors, it would still be a very serious breach of Catholic discipline to decline obstinately the direction of those who have received from heaven the mission to guide individuals and communities along the straight path of truth and goodness."[17] Traditionalists claim they are simply worshiping the way the Church has always worshiped and practicing their faith the way their ancestors always did. Even if this is true, conducting a ministry of this sort in universal and obstinate opposition to the Church's apostolic authority, which is essential to its existence, is simply indefensible.

---

[17] Pius X, *Notre Charge Apostolique* (1910), Papal Encyclicals Online, https://www.papalencyclicals.net/pius10/p10notre.htm

8.

Bishops Against Bishops

Thus far, I have established the following. Traditionalist clergy lack any legitimate mission, ordinary or extraordinary. The Church has explicitly condemned their appeal to a "state of necessity." Supplied jurisdiction is based either on personal intention or absolute universality, both of which are objectively fallacious conclusions that reveal an equally fallacious premise. No ministry can be undertaken apart from and in opposition to the Church's lawful shepherds, as Christ Himself confirmed. Their ministry simply lacks foundation.

With the structural supports of traditionalism addressed, it is now necessary to examine the ramifications of their ministry. What if their position were indeed correct? The first thing to address, then, is episcopacy, and what would need to be admitted regarding its nature if the traditionalist position were a legitimate one.

Traditionalists often appeal to dire warnings from Marian apparitions as justifications for their actions. Among them is the prophecy of Our Lady of Akita, in which she gave a warning that should give us pause after understanding the traditionalist ministry. She said, "The work of the devil will infiltrate even into the Church in such a way that one will see cardinals opposing cardinals, bishops

against bishops."[1] Traditionalists will often point at the strife between bishops who appear to have differing levels of orthodoxy as
proof of this prophecy's fulfillment. But is that all it means?

An examination of the episcopal office is first in order. There are
two intertwined facets of Holy Orders; the spiritual component,
manifested in the Eucharist and the necessary connection it has to
the indelible mark of priestly ordination, and the juridical component, manifested in authority that is exercised and delegated. As
Pope Pius XII wrote in his encyclical *Mystici Corporis Christi*, "[T]he
invisible mission of the Holy spirit and the juridical commission of
Ruler and Teacher received from Christ...mutually complement
and perfect each other - as do the body and soul in man - and proceed from our one Redeemer who not only said as He breathed on
the Apostles 'Receive ye the Holy Spirit,' but also clearly com-
manded: 'As the Father hath sent me, I also send you;' and again:
'He that heareth you, heareth me.'"[2] These two truths are the basis
for sacramental communion and ecclesial communion.

Episcopal power is innately connected to the Eucharist and
therefore to the communion of the Church as a whole. Joseph
Ratzinger wrote that a bishop's consecration creates a "direct sacramental root" that is intrinsically bound to the "sacramental actual-
ity" of the college of bishops, and is never taken as "a merely indi-

---

[1] John Ata, "A Message From Our Lady - Akita, Japan," EWTN.
https://www.ewtn.com/catholicism/library/message-from-our-lady--
akita-japan-5167

[2] Pius XII, *Mystici Corporis Christi* (1943), Vatican Archive,
https://www.vatican.va/content/pius-xii/en/encyclicals/documents/hf_p-
xii_enc_29061943_mystici-corporis-christi.html

vidual gift, but relates to the living unity of the Church as an organism."[3] He further explains that in the Middle Ages an unfortunate theological rift had separated the spiritual power of Holy Orders from its associated governance, creating an erroneous distinction between sacramental communion and juridical communion. The common belief was that the celebration of the sacraments, centered on the real Body of Christ in the Eucharist, ran parallel with the Church's juridical structure, or the Mystical Body of Christ. "Thus the legal sphere became completely independent in the Church alongside the sacramental sphere,"[4] as Ratzinger wrote, and thus the connection between the Eucharist and the unity of the Church was diminished.

This unfortunately opened the door to a deficient understanding of Holy Orders that prioritized the juridical aspect over the spiritual, and individualized sacramental rituals. But the power granted by Christ to the apostles and their successors is not merely administrative, as if the Church were a governmental body or a humanly constructed entity. As Leo XIII stated in *Satis cognitum*, "[J]ust as it is necessary that the authority of Peter should be perpetuated in the Roman Pontiff, so, by the fact that the bishops succeed the Apostles, they inherit their ordinary power, and thus the episcopal order necessarily belongs to the essential constitution of the Church."[5] Notice that the pontiff refers to the episcopal *order*, not simply episcopal power. The divinely appointed authority of the bishops only makes sense in the context of the college of bishops as an undivided whole.

---

[3] Ratzinger, *Theological Highlights of Vatican II*, 187.

[4] Ibid., 188.

[5] Leo XIII, *Satis cognitum*.

To apply this to the traditionalists, the historical divide between the governing power in the Church and the sacramental power of Holy Orders may give some context for their defense of adhering to "Eternal Rome," finding it necessary to separate from "temporal Rome" until such time as it "returns to Tradition."[6] They act as though the spiritual, invisible church can exist independently of the physical, visible church, and that if "temporal Rome" falters, maintaining fidelity to "Eternal Rome" will revive it. Pope Pius XII strongly condemned this in his encyclical on the Mystical Body of Christ, in which he wrote the following:

> From what We have thus far written, and explained, Venerable Brethren, it is clear, We think, how grievously they err who arbitrarily claim that the Church is something hidden and invisible, as they also do who look upon her as a mere human institution possession a certain disciplinary code and external ritual, but lacking power to communicate supernatural life. [...] For this reason We deplore and condemn the pernicious error of those who dream of an imaginary Church, a kind of society that finds its origin and growth in charity, to which, somewhat contemptuously, they oppose another, which they call juridical.[7]

His predecessor Leo XIII also wrote in *Satis cognitum*:

---

[6] See Archbishop Lefebvre's remarks in his 1988 consecration homily here: https://sspx.org/en/1988-episcopal-consecrations-sermon-of-archbishop-lefebvre

[7] Pius XII, *Mystici Corporis Christi*.

It is assuredly as impossible that the Church of Jesus Christ can be the one or the other, as that man should be a body alone or a soul alone. The connection and union of both elements is as absolutely necessary to the true Church as the intimate union of the soul and body is to human nature. As Christ, the Head and Exemplar, is not wholly in His visible human nature, which Photinians and Nestorians assert, nor wholly in the invisible divine nature, as the Monophysites hold, but is one, from and in both natures, visible and invisible; so the mystical body of Christ is the true Church, only because its visible parts draw life and power from the supernatural gifts and other things whence spring their very nature and essence.[8]

The issue is that episcopal power, by its very *nature*, cannot be exercised in any form of independence or opposition. Doing so would keep the governing power and the spiritual power separate and would necessarily imply a conflict between the visible and invisible church. It wrenches the unity of the Eucharist away from its greater ecclesial context. Episcopal power is not merely a means to an end; that reduces its amazing spiritual power to base functionality.

This, however, is precisely what traditionalism has made of the office of the bishop, and subsequently of the priesthood. It strips Holy Orders of its most elemental meaning. Traditionalist bishops are not ordained to promote the unity and communion of the Body. They are ordained for precisely the opposite reason—so that the

---

[8] Leo XIII, *Satis cognitum.*

people will have recourse to bishops who are "truly traditional" and who can "make priests" that are of the same caliber. They serve the organization and their own ideology, not the church as a whole. They have taken the sacramental core of the episcopacy and reduced it to a mere function, and "use" it to establish a ministry directly contrary to the lawful shepherds. It is, without a doubt, an abuse of the sacrament to confer Holy Orders for the sole purpose of continuing an apostolate that is completely independent of any other church.

Canon 375 §2 says the following: "Through episcopal consecration itself, bishops receive with the function of sanctifying also the functions of teaching and governing; *by their nature, however, these can only be exercised in hierarchical communion with the head and members of the college.*"[9] Pope Pius XII said much the same thing in his allocution *Si diligis* at the canonization of Pope St. Pius X: "Those who are so called teach not in their own name, nor by reason of their theological knowledge, but by reason of the mandate which they have received from the lawful Teaching Authority. Their faculty always remains subject to that Authority, *nor is it ever exercised in its own right or independently.*"[10] Bishops certainly have individual authority over their appointed dioceses, but just as one diocese cannot be in conflict with another in juridical terms, one bishop cannot be in conflict with another in spiritual terms. As Joseph Ratzinger

---

[9] 1983 Code of Canon Law, c. 375 §2, in *Code of Canon Law*, Vatican Archive, https://www.vatican.va/archive/cod-iuris-canonici/eng/documents/cic_lib2-cann368-430_en.html

[10] Pius XII, *Si diligis - Canonisation of St. Pius X* (1954), Papal Encyclicals Online, https://www.papalencyclicals.net/pius12/p12sidil.htm

wrote, "[A]lthough the local Church structure is a totality in itself, it is not sufficient unto itself. In its structure as an individual parish it is, so to speak, open-ended. It is complete only when the bishop does not stand alone, but is himself in communion with the other bishops of the other Churches of God."[11]

The relationship between the spiritual and the temporal is absolutely indispensable for the life of the Church. As Joseph Ratzinger further wrote, episcopal orders given individually and exercised apart from the rest of the college of bishops makes the sacrament "restricted to a liturgical-juridical formalism," and that episcopal ordination is not a rite "by which one can bypass the rest of the Church and dig one's own private channel to the apostles. It is, rather, an expression of the continuity of the church, which, in the communion of bishops, is the locus of tradition, of the Gospel of Jesus Christ."[12] Isolating the power of the bishop leads to such disastrous results as the consecrations performed by Archbishop Ngô Đình Thục, a Vietnamese sedevacantist bishop who reconciled with Rome before his death, but who left behind an episcopal line which is absolutely incomprehensible.[13]

Naturally, since the two facets of Holy Orders are so intimately connected, a misuse of the spiritual element will have repercussions in the sphere of ecclesiastical governance, leading to competing

---

[11] Ratzinger, *Theological Highlights of Vatican II*, 179.

[12] Ratzinger, *Principles of Catholic Theology*, 246.

[13] A flowchart of sedevacantist ordinations and clergy can be found here: https://ia902606.us.archive.org/5/items/bbb_20230630/magna_carta_05-20-2020.pdf

ministries and apostolates when independent bishops delegate independent priests. As previous chapters have discussed, the ministry of the Church cannot be directed in opposition to itself; one cannot claim to be truly fulfilling the role of a priest or bishop if he is giving himself a mission over a flock which has already been delegated to another. As Rev. Walter Devivier said, "To belong to the legitimate line of the pastors of the Church, or to the hierarchy of jurisdiction, it is not enough that a Bishop should have received the power of Orders; he must have received besides the mission or authorization to govern a diocese. [...] He must therefore have subjects on whom to exercise his authority or governing power. *But one cannot give himself subjects.*"[14]

Supposing the traditionalist position is correct, and another bishop and his priests enter a diocese that has not been delegated to them, what gives them authority over the faithful there? Has the ordinary bishop's jurisdiction been revoked? Can a new shepherd enter the sheepfold and assume control over the flock? And what if yet another vagus bishop comes? If, for example, the SSPX ministers in a location under supplied jurisdiction, as they believe the ordinary pastors are "compromised," and then another independent group claims the same supplied jurisdiction to minister to the same flock, on the basis that the SSPX is "compromised" (as, for example, the Resistance believes), who is the rightful shepherd? Can the laity simply pick from an array of available ministers based on their personal preferences?

---

[14] Walter Devivier, S.J., *Christian Apologetics, Volume II*. Translated, edited, and augmented by Rev. Joseph Sasia, S.J. (New York: Wagner, 1924), 33-34 (emphasis in original).

Surely, it is clear that the Church cannot be sustained in this way, with bishops and priests vying for ministerial power over a flock which has not been delegated to them. As stated previously, a lawful mission is necessary; bishops and priests cannot simply present themselves as one of several options that the laity can decide among for what best fits their needs. The Church would possess no real authority if this were the case. As Pope Leo XIII further wrote in *Satis cognitum*:

> [W]e must note that the due order of things and their mutual relations are disturbed if there be a twofold magistracy of the same rank set over a people, neither of which is amenable to the other. [...] "It is not congruous that two superiors with equal authority should be placed over the same flock; but that two, one of whom is higher than the other, should be placed over the same people is not incongruous. Thus the parish priest, the bishop, and the Pope, are placed immediately over the same people" (St. Thomas in iv Sent, dist. xvii., a. 4, ad q. 4, ad 3).[15]

This is why the eventual reality of the SSPX needing to consecrate new bishops really amounts to nothing. They will have another bishop who can validly ordain priests, but he does not have the authority to send those priests to minister anywhere. He fulfills a function or a role, nothing more. He is not in communion with his fellow bishops and sends priests to minister in their fold without their consent. There is a rumor that Bishop Fellay of the SSPX has been

---

[15] Leo XIII, *Satis cognitum*.

granted permission by the Holy See to ordain priests, but even if this is true, he has no jurisdiction over them and cannot grant them any jurisdiction.

Can it be said that the traditionalists are mending the confusion and turmoil in the Church if they are intruding into dioceses and assigning themselves a flock while claiming that the lawful authorities are compromised? Does this not simply compound the confusion? How could divine law ever permit two opposing authorities to both be legitimate when their very power comes from the unity and oneness of the Eucharist and is directed toward fostering the unity of the Church? This is a contradiction and would imply that the Church (and therefore the Lord) could sanction division or disunity. As Rev. Gerard Van Noort wrote, in a scenario in which God granted apostolic power to men who were not in union with the ordinary apostolic successors, "there would be two separate and independent sources of authority, both demanding, by divine right, obedience from the same subjects. *The only thing that could result in such an hypothesis would be confusion and schism in Christ's Church.* And in that event, one would imply that God Himself, who willed His Church to be unified, was Himself sowing the seeds of necessary division."[16]

As with mission, jurisdiction, and apostolic authority, historical precedent is once again crucial for understanding the gravity of this law. Territorial delegation is not something that evolved, or that went into force when the Church became more global and established new dioceses; it has been part of her teaching since the very

---

[16] Gerard Van Noort, *Dogmatic Theology, Volume II: Christ's Church* (Westminster; Newman Press, 1957), 154.

beginning. Consider the following declarations from previous councils, whose binding authority is never disputed amongst traditionalists. It is quite clear that overlapping ministries and vying prelates are not conducive to the proper order and unity of the Body of Christ.

The First Council of Constantinople (381 AD) declared in Canon 2: "Diocesan bishops are not to intrude in churches beyond their own boundaries nor are they to confuse the churches... Unless invited, bishops are not to go outside their diocese to perform an ordination or any other ecclesiastical business."[17]

The Fourth Council of Constantinople (869-70 AD) declared in Canon 23: "[T]his great and universal synod has decided that no brother of ours in the episcopate or anyone else may ...install priests or any other clerics in churches that are not under his jurisdiction, without the permission of the bishop responsible for the church in question. Furthermore, no priests or deacons, who are consecrated for holy functions, should perform, of their own accord and decision, any sacred functions in churches to which they have not been appointed from the beginning. This behaviour is unlawful and utterly alien to the canonical regulations."[18]

The Council of Trent (1545-63 AD) declared in Session VI: "It shall not be lawful for any bishop, under the plea of any privilege [what]soever, to exercise pontifical functions in the diocese of another, save by the express permission of the Ordinary of the place,

---

[17] First Council of Constantinople - 381, Canon 2, Papal Encyclicals Online, https://www.papalencyclicals.net/councils/ecum02.htm

[18] Fourth Council of Constantinople: 869-870, Canon 23, Papal Encyclicals Online, https://www.papalencyclicals.net/councils/ecum08.htm

and in regard to those persons only who are subject to that same Ordinary: if the contrary shall have been done, the bishop shall be ipso facto suspended from the exercise of episcopal functions, and those so ordained (be similarly suspended) from the exercise of their orders."[19]

True Catholic tradition is abundantly clear on the matter. No bishop can exercise his power independently or in opposition to his brother bishops; this is contrary to the very essence of episcopal authority, and all bishops who entered the fold of another without lawful delegation have been denounced as intruders in the Church's past. St. Francis de Sales defends the church's order with the following passage: "And how could that be a united flock which should be led by two shepherds, unknown to each other, into different pastures, with different calls and folds, and each of them expecting to have the whole. Thus would it be with the Church under a variety of pastors...dragged hither and thither into various sects."[20]

Can there be "one flock" and "one shepherd," as Our Lord prayed there would be, if the flock can simply choose its own shepherd from an available multitude, or if the same shepherds seize the flocks that have been given to another? The Church's constant teaching compels us to refuse this proposition and again give our assent to the teaching that despite all potential hardships, the laity have a duty to submit to their legitimate shepherds and to refuse any others who demand their obedience.

---

[19] General Council of Trent: Sixth Session, Decree on Reformation, Chapter V, Papal Encyclicals Online, https://www.papalencyclicals.net/councils/trent/sixth-session.htm

[20] Sales, *The Catholic Controversy*, 11.

9.

Refusal of Communion

The subject of schism is among the most hotly debated topics in traditionalist circles, especially among the SSPX as they represent the public face of the movement. Despite Pope St. John Paul II's warning the faithful that "formal adherence to the schism [of Lefebvre] is a grave offense against God,"[1] the subsequent confirmation from the Pontifical Council for the Interpretation of Legislative Texts in 1996 which stated that "[a]s long as there are no changes which may lead to the re-establishment of this necessary communion, the whole Lefebvrian movement is to be held schismatic, in view of the existence of a formal declaration by the Supreme Authority on this matter,"[2] and Pope Francis' affirmation of this in his letter

---

[1] John Paul II, *Ecclesia Dei*.

[2] The Pontifical Council for the Interpretation of Legislative Texts, "The Excommunication of Followers of Archbishop Lefebvre," August 24, 1996, Catholic Culture. https://www.catholicculture.org/culture/library/view.cfm?recnum=1224 (original in Italian here: https://www.vatican.va/roman_curia/pontifical_councils/intrptxt/documents/rc_pc_intrptxt_doc_19960824_vescovo -lefebvre_it.html). Supporters of the SSPX will object that this statement no longer applies because it was issued before Pope Benedict XVI lifted the excommunications of the four SSPX bishops in 2009. There are a number of problems with this argument, however. Firstly, it would concede that they *were* in schism beforehand for twenty years. Secondly, the SSPX has done nothing differently since 2009; in fact, they have only persisted in their contumacy. If the declared schism was nullified when the excommunications were lifted, this would mean that schism is merely a status that is contingent on a penal declaration,

that accompanied *Traditionis custodes,* in which he stated that Pope Benedict's previous permissions for the Latin Mass were "to foster the healing of the schism with the movement of Mons. Lefebvre,"[3] the traditionalists claim that they are not in schism, they never have been, and that it is offensive and slanderous to say otherwise.

As stated in the introduction, this is not a matter that will be settled by presenting an array of quotes and trying to reconcile them. There are many canon lawyers, priests, and bishops who have given their opinion on this subject, and for each one arguing in defense of the traditionalists, another can be found that argues the opposite. There should be no appeal after such definitive declarations listed above, issued from the Holy See itself (declarations that were intended for the entire Church and are not alleged quotes from private

---

unrelated to any action on the part of the recipient. If an organization commits a transgression and incurs a penalty, and persists in their transgression after the penalty is lifted, is the transgression suddenly gone? One does not need to be excommunicated to be in a state of schism (as in the case of the Orthodox). One also has to wonder how the schism could vanish upon lifting the excommunications if John Paul II warned against formal adherence to the schism as a movement (one cannot formally adhere to an episcopal consecration). It should be noted, this declaration clarifies that one is not a *de facto* schismatic simply because they attend an SSPX chapel, but that holding positions contrary to the Magisterium and exclusively attending these chapels would likely constitute "formal adherence."

[3] Francis, "Letter of the Holy Father Francis to the bishops of the whole world, that accompanies the Apostolic Letter motu proprio data Traditionis custodes," July 16, 2021, Vatican Archive, https://www.vatican.va/content/francesco/en/letters/2021/documents/20210716-lettera-vescovi-liturgia.html

conversations), but as the subject continues to generate debate, it is worth examining the core of the matter.

Schism is defined in Canon 751 of the 1983 Code (Canon 1325 §2 of the 1917 Code) as "the refusal of submission to the Roman Pontiff, or refusal of communion with the members of the church subject to him."[4] The Recognize and Resist traditionalists claim they cannot be schismatic because they submit to the authority of the papacy, but they believe the popes since Vatican II have operated outside the scope of that authority or have acted "contrary to Tradition," and that it is simply necessary to operate independently until such time as the Church "returns to Tradition." In their words, they "resist the present ecclesiastical orientation in order to remain in the one Church of Christ," and that "it is to remain obedient to the invisible Head of the Church that [we] resist the present-day orientation"[5] (a position decisively condemned by Pope Pius XII in *Mystici Corporis Christi*). In the case of the sedevacantists, they say they cannot be schismatics because, quite simply, there is no pope, and if there were one, they would absolutely submit to him.

After sifting through their defenses against schism, one notices a pattern. They almost exclusively respond to the first part of the canonical definition. It is very telling that they rarely, if ever, address the clause about refusal of communion with those subject to the

---

[4] 1983 Code of Canon Law, c. 751, in *Code of Canon Law*, Vatican Archive. https://www.vatican.va/archive/cod-iuris-canonici/eng/documents/cic_lib3-cann747-755_en.html#BOOK_III

[5] "Neither schismatic nor excommunicated," SSPX Website. https://sspx.org/en/neither-schismatic-nor-excommunicated-30934

Pope. How would one refuse communion? Or perhaps to begin more simply, what is communion?

This answer should be obvious to us as Catholics. Communion is the Eucharist. But this often gets reduced to a more particular understanding of the word. For example, to "receive communion" does not simply mean to consume the Eucharistic elements. It means to enter into communion with the Mystical Body. It means to partake of the Body and Blood of Christ, which in turn unites us all to our fellow Catholics to bind the unity of the Body of Christ together as a living Body. As St. Paul wrote, "Because there is one bread, we who are many are one body, for we all partake of the one bread" (1 Cor 10:17).

Eucharistic communion is inseparable from ecclesial communion, as the previous chapter made clear. Just as it would be nonsensical to attempt to construct the Church without the Eucharist, perhaps by simply gathering together and professing the same beliefs, as if to conjure up the Church by our own efforts instead of receiving it from Christ, we cannot demand the Eucharist without the rest of the Church. They are so intimately linked that to separate them is to wrench a spiritual unity from a physical unity, or vice versa. Joseph Ratzinger wrote the following: "The Church is communion, communion with the whole Body of Christ. Expressed in different terms: In the Eucharist I can never demand communion with Jesus alone. He has given himself a Body. Whoever receives him in communion necessarily communicates with all his brothers and sisters who have become members of the one Body."[6]

So, with the definition clearly laid out, what does it mean to refuse communion? It is quite simple, if we have a grasp of Catholic tradition. Refusing communion means refusing to worship in common with others, and subsequently refusing to act as part of a cohesive whole. It means setting oneself apart, making one's own church an isolated and exclusive entity that is a gathering of those who hold a common ideology, but not a gathering of the whole Church. To be in communion ultimately means to become "one body." We are in communion with each other by being drawn into the Body of Christ as a whole, which starts with celebrating the Eucharist together as a whole, not as individuals or as communities set apart from others. What is communion if not the Eucharist? And what is a refusal of communion if not a refusal to celebrate the Eucharist, the very sacrament of unity, with the rest of the Church?

St. Paul further writes to the Corinthians, "As it is, there are many parts, yet one body. The eye cannot say to the hand, 'I have no need of you,' nor again the head to the feet, 'I have no need of you.'" (1 Cor 12:20-21). With some words substituted, the traditionalists cannot say to the local Catholic church, "I have no need of you," nor again the priest to the local bishop, "I have no need of you." Celebrating the Eucharist while actively denouncing all other Catholics is antithetical to the very idea of communion. As Pope Benedict XVI wrote:

---

[6] Joseph Ratzinger, *Called to Communion: Understanding the Church Today,* trans. Adrian Walker (San Francisco; Ignatius Press, 1996), 82.

But in all places, Christ is only one, and on that account we cannot receive him against others or without others. Precisely because it is the whole Christ, the undivided and indivisible Christ, who gives himself in the Eucharist, for that very reason the Eucharist can be celebrated rightly only if it is celebrated with the whole Church. We have Christ only if we have him together with others. Because the Eucharist is concerned only with Christ, it is a sacrament of the Church. And for the same reason it can be carried on only in unity with the whole Church and with her authority.[7]

And how would one celebrate the Eucharist "against others or without others?" By separating oneself from the rest of the Body. By worshiping opposed to the lawful authority of the Church, or by refusing to worship outside one's selective group or ideology. Rejecting the authority of the bishops and separating oneself from the Church as a whole results in exclusive worship on one's own terms. This is what Catholic tradition refers to as "rival altars."

Several Church fathers have written on this topic and mince no words about the gravity of this error. St. Cyprian of Carthage, in his extensive work *On the Unity of the Church*, condemns in no uncertain terms the presbyter who "dares to set up another altar, to make another prayer with unauthorized words, to profane the truth of the

---

[7] Ratzinger, *God Is Near Us*, 120.

Lord's offering by false sacrifices," calling him "a disobedient servant, an impious son, a hostile brother[.]"[8] St. Ignatius of Antioch, in
the second century AD, wrote to the Philadelphians, "Take heed,
then, to have but one Eucharist. For there is one flesh of our Lord
Jesus Christ, and one cup to [show forth] the unity of His blood; one
altar; as there is one bishop[.]"[9] He also wrote to the Ephesians, "He,
therefore, that does not assemble with the Church, has even by this
manifested his pride, and condemned himself."[10]

St. Augustine held back no words about the offense of rival altars
and did not hesitate to identify it as a sign of schism. In one letter,
he says, "What we dislike in that party is not their bearing with those
who are wicked, but their intolerable wickedness in the matter of
schism, of raising altar against altar," and again references this when
he says they are guilty of schism who are "stained with the atrocious
crime of having actually reared their rival altar[.]"[11] In another letter,
he writes, "For some of your predecessors, in whose impious schism
you obstinately remain, ...then set up a bishop against the ordained
bishop, and erected an altar against the altar already recognised."[12]

---

[8] Cyprian of Carthage, *On the Unity of the Church*, 17, retrieved from
New Advent, https://www.newadvent.org/fathers/050701.htm

[9] Ignatius of Antioch, *The Epistle of Ignatius to the Philadelphians*, Ch.
4, retrieved from New Advent, https://www.newadvent.org/fa-
thers/0108.htm

[10] Ignatius of Antioch, *The Epistle of Ignatius to the Ephesians*, Ch. 5,
retrieved from New Advent, https://www.newadvent.org/fathers/
0104.htm

[11] Augustine, Letter 43 (A.D. 397), Ch. 8, retrieved from new Advent,
https://www.newadvent.org/fathers/1102043.htm

[12] Augustine, Letter 76 (A.D. 402), retrieved from New Advent,
https://www.newadvent.org/fathers/1102076.htm

In his letter to Patilian the Donatist, he said that those who pretend not to see the errors of the schismatic Donatus "openly sever themselves; they openly erect altar against altar."[13]

St. Gregory of Nyssa writes a particularly applicable passage in one of his letters: "And what means this opposing array of new Altars? Do we announce another Jesus? Do we hint at another? Do we produce other scriptures? [...] What charge like these can be brought against us, that our company should be reckoned a thing to be avoided, and that in some places another altar should be erected in opposition to us, as if we should defile their sanctuaries?"[14]

His questions can be overlaid onto the present context quite easily. What is meant by an array of unauthorized altars throughout the world, built by the traditionalists where they have not been given the jurisdiction to do so? Does the Church "announce another Jesus" or produce novel teachings through her declarations of the Council, such that she and her followers ought to be avoided? Should other independent altars be built in opposition to the lawful ones, as if "Novus Ordo Catholics" would "defile the sanctuaries" of traditionalists?

Returning briefly to the topic of mission, St. Francis de Sales also has words regarding the possibility of extraordinary mission and its legitimacy regarding worship. He says that an extraordinary mission is never legitimate where it opposes or conflicts with the ordinary mission of the Church. "Witness all the Prophets, who never set up

---

[13] Augustine, *Answer to Petilian the Donatist (Book I)*, Ch. 24, retrieved from New Advent, https://www.newadvent.org/fathers/14091.htm

[14] Gregory of Nyssa, Letter 17, retrieved from New Advent, https://www.newadvent.org/fathers/291117.htm

altar against altar, never overthrew the priesthood of Aaron, never abolished the constitutions of the Synagogue. Witness Our Lord, who declares that every kingdom divided against itself shall be brought to desolation, and a house upon a house shall fall (Luke xi. 17)."[15]

In 1997, ex-SSPX priest Robert Neville admitted to the same conclusion in his letter explaining his reasons for leaving the Society:

> If [John Paul II] is the pope, then the masses offered by the priests of the Society of St. Pius X mentioning his name in the Canon are schismatic, because they are offered outside of and even against his authority. If this is the case, the Society is raising its altars against the altar of the Vicar of Christ, which is certainly a schismatic act. [...] Its priests celebrate Mass and hear confessions in defiance of the bishops who have been appointed by John Paul II. If these bishops truly have authority over the various dioceses, how can that authority be recognized, but at the same time not obeyed? If John Paul II and the hierarchy in communion with him have authority and jurisdiction, then the Society of St. Pius X is raising its altars against the altar of the Vicar of Christ.[16]

---

[15] Sales, *The Catholic Controversy*, 13.

[16] Fr Robert L. Neville to Bishop Bernard Fellay, December 17, 1997, *Why Do Priests Leave the SSPX?* https://www.tapatalk.com/groups/ignis_ardens/viewtopic.php?f=11&t= 11560&sid=7bde664ef4a544b05fb9a-1924a9c57db&view=print

Traditionalists will declare that the Mass the lawful bishop and his priests offer is offensive to God at best, and invalid at worst. They will refuse to attend or participate in it and will discourage others from doing so. They will not worship with their local Catholic neighbors even if they worship according to the same liturgical books as them, and they will refuse to receive communion if circumstances like a funeral or wedding demand they attend (I have attended multiple weddings at FSSP chapels in which SSPX adherents in the congregation refused to receive the Eucharist, and this is not a case of one or two extremists; in one instance, an entire half of the church who were relatives of the bride did not receive). They will drive several hours to a Latin Mass, passing who knows how many churches along the way, and even deliberately miss Mass on a regular basis if the organization they adhere to can only send a priest out once or twice a month to their mission chapel. One independent traditionalist chapel even asks visitors that they "do not come forward for Communion until [they] decide to assist at the traditional Latin Mass exclusively and to refrain from ever attending the New Mass of Pope Paul VI, even for funerals and weddings."[17]

But their position is not only based on inferences; they offer quite explicit proof of refusing common worship. In Fr. Matthias Gaudron's book *The Catechism of the Crisis of the Church*, he states that if one must attend the Novus Ordo Missae for "family or pro-

---

[17] Our Lady of the Pillar Traditional Catholic Chapel, "Dress Code & Communion Policy," olpchapel.org. https://olpchapel.org/when-you-visit/dress-code-communion-policy/

fessional reasons," that "of course, one does not go to Communion."[18] Elsewhere, they go so far as to compare it to idol worship, substituting words into St. Paul's admonishments from 1 Corinthians (the very same letter that warns against divisions in the Church) to describe the "scandal" of attending the Novus Ordo Missae: "'Because if someone sees you, you who have knowledge, seated at a table in the idol's temple' (today we would say at the table of the Conciliar supper), 'shall not his conscience, being weak, bring him' to attend and to receive Communion at the New Mass? 'And through thy knowledge shall you sin thus against the brethren, and wound their weak conscience, you sin against Christ.'"[19] In several books published by the SSPX, *Christian Warfare* and *Retreat Manual and Family Prayer Book*, the examinations of conscience have the following entry listed under sins against the 3rd Commandment: "Have you attended and actively participated in the 'New Mass'?" Their website also directly states that "Catholics are not obliged to attend the *Novus Ordo* as it puts the faith in danger," and that "whoever is conscious of this danger…commits a sin against faith [by attending the [Novus Ordo Missae]]."[20]

They not only refuse communion with their fellow Catholics; they teach and believe that it is a sin! That it is an offense to Our

---

[18] Matthias Gaudron, *The Catechism of the Crisis of the Church* (Kansas City; Angelus Press, 2010), 153

[19] Fr. Van Es, "Attendance at Today's Masses," Society of St Pius X - District of Asia. https://www.sspxasia.com/Documents/Sacraments/Attendance_at_Todays_Masses.htm

[20] "Must Catholics attend the New Mass?" SSPX website. https://sspx.org/en/must-catholics-attend-new-mass

Lord to participate in the very act that confirms our communion with His Mystical Body! To claim it is a sin to commune with the faithful who are subject to the Pope is essentially to claim it is a sin to be Catholic! Lest anyone think this is merely inflammatory rhetoric, a former priest of the SSPX cited the same conclusion as one of his reasons for leaving them: "It is, we say, objectively a sin to receive, give or assist at Novus Ordo rites…(the consequence indeed, which we refuse to formulate in actual words, is that it is sinful to have a juridical relationship with the Pope and the College of Bishops—hence our condemnation of the Indult, St. Peter's, etc.)."[21]

I understand not every traditionalist holds this opinion, but it is a fact that it is circulated in their publications. Even if they do not explicitly say it is a sin to attend, they claim the Novus Ordo Missae is offensive to God, that it is harmful to one's faith, and ought to be avoided at all costs, even if it means failing to fulfill one's Sunday obligation. What does this describe if not sin?

And yet despite all this, the "Recognize and Resist" traditionalists will claim they are in fact in communion with the Church and the local bishop, on the sole basis that their priest says his name and acknowledges him during the Mass, as the rubrics of the canon stipulate. This, I believe, demonstrates a severely deficient understanding of the idea of communion. As St. Ignatius of Antioch wrote to the Magnesians, "It is fitting, then, not only to be called Christians, but to be so in reality: *as some indeed give one the title of bishop, but do all things without him.* Now such persons seem to me to be not

---

[21] Campbell, letter to Bishop Bernard Fellay.

possessed of a good conscience, seeing they are not [steadfastly] gathered together according to the commandment."[22]

The wondrous spiritual reality of communion in the Church cannot be achieved simply by pronouncing a bishop's name at a prescribed time while offering the sacrifice without the approval of that bishop they are naming. If it were that simple, communion is no more than a legalistic delineation that is dependent on imposed rubrics, rather than a sacramental reality. And the Church is not a temporal structure held together by legalism. The Church is the Body of Christ, a reality manifested by His perfect sacrifice which loses its meaning when offered in a contradictory manner. Priests are not in communion with the local bishop if they ignore him except when the rubrics of their liturgy require them to acknowledge him, and the faithful are not in communion with the rest of the Church if they will not worship at any other church or with any other congregation.

St. Ignatius of Antioch also wrote to the Smyrnaeans, "Let that be deemed a proper Eucharist, which is [administered] either by the bishop, or by one to whom he has entrusted it."[23] Here he affirms the necessity of jurisdiction in relation to the celebration of the Eucharist. Only the bishop or those he has sent can legitimately celebrate the Eucharist because celebrating it outside of these criteria does not maintain authentic communion. If the Church's mark of "One" is established by the institution of the Eucharist and maintained through its perpetual celebration, both of which are made

---

[22] Ignatius of Antioch, *The Epistle of Ignatius to the Magnesians*, Ch. 4, retrieved from New Advent, https://www.newadvent.org/fathers/0105.htm

[23] *The Epistle of Ignatius to the Smyrneans*, Ch. 8.

possible by the divine authority of the bishops, then offering this sacrament of unity outside of the Church's juridical structure can only be seen as a contradictory offering. As Pope St. John Paul II wrote in *Ecclesia de Eucharistia*: "The Bishop, in effect, is the visible principle and the foundation of unity within his particular Church. It would therefore be a great contradiction if the sacrament *par excellence* of the Church's unity were celebrated without true communion with the Bishop."[24] Pope Benedict XVI had very similar words in his book *God Is Near Us*: "[T]he mentioning of the bishop and the pope by name, in the celebration of the Eucharist, is not merely an external matter, but an inner necessity of that celebration. […] *For this reason the Mass needs the person who does not speak in his own name, who does not come on his own authority, but who represents the whole Church*[.]"[25]

The case of the sedevacantists is so explicit it merits little examination. Sedevacantists will celebrate what are known as non-*una cum* Masses. This refers to the prayer in the Canon where the priest names the pope with the prayer "*una cum famulo tuo Papa nostro (N),*" or "together with your servant, (N), our Pope." They deliberately omit this clause, which should leave no doubt as to whether this confirms a refusal of communion. Fr. Anthony Cekada, a sedevacantist priest, explicitly stated that to participate in a Mass that

---

[24] John Paul II, *Ecclesia de Eucharistia* (2003), Vatican Archive, https://www.vatican.va/content/john-paul-ii/en/encyclicals/documents/hf_jp-ii_enc_20030417_eccl-de-euch.html (emphasis in original)

[25] Ratzinger, *God is Near Us*, 53 (emphasis in original)

includes the "una cum" clause means that one "[p]rofesses communion with heretics"[26] and is comparable to offering a grain of incense to pagan gods.

A final passage from Pope Benedict XVI is worth examining for the context of this chapter:

> Anyone who does not celebrate the Eucharist with everyone is merely creating a caricature of it. The Eucharist is celebrated with the one Christ, and thus with the whole Church, or it is not being celebrated at all. Anyone who is only looking for his own group or clique in the Eucharist…is, so to say, sitting down with his back to the others and is thus annihilating the Eucharist for himself and spoiling it for the others. He is then just holding his own meal and is despising the Churches of God (I Cor 11:21f.).[27]

While it cannot be denied that there was a stronger emphasis on the Eucharist as a meal in the years immediately following the Second Vatican Council, a casual celebration or misunderstanding of its sacrificial nature is not the only way to reduce its meaning. Some may have indeed worshiped with this deficient understanding of the Eucharist, but they nonetheless celebrated it in union with their lawful pastor and the lawful bishop, maintaining the ecclesial communion that is so integral to the sacrament. Are the traditionalists able

---

[26] Anthony Cekada, "The Grain of Incense: Sedevacantists and Una Cum Masses," November 2007, traditionalmass.org. https://www.traditionalmass.org/images/articles/SedesUnCum.pdf

[27] Ratzinger, *Pilgrim Fellowship of Faith*, 106.

to criticize this when they receive Jesus in opposition to the rest of the Church, demanding physical communion while rejecting ecclesial communion and likewise celebrating it merely as a "meal" among those who agree with them? They may be adorning their ceremonies with all the pomp and circumstance they can muster, but they are nevertheless indeed looking for "their own group or clique" in the Eucharist and prioritizing their ideology over full communion with Jesus Christ and the Church as one living Body.

St. Irenaeus wrote the following on the necessity of fraternal communion as part of the sacrifice:

> For at the beginning God had respect to the gifts of Abel, because he offered with single-mindedness and righteousness; but He had no respect unto the offering of Cain, because his heart was divided with envy and malice, which he cherished against his brother, as God says when reproving his hidden [thoughts], Though you offer rightly, yet, if you do not divide rightly, have you not sinned? Be at rest; since God is not appeased by sacrifice. For if any one shall endeavour to offer a sacrifice merely to outward appearance, unexceptionably, in due order, and according to appointment, while in his soul he does not assign to his neighbour that fellowship with him which is right and proper, nor is under the fear of God —he who thus cherishes secret sin does not deceive God by that sacrifice which is offered correctly as to outward appearance; nor will such an oblation profit him anything, but [only] the giving up of that evil which has been conceived within him,

so that sin may not the more, by means of the hypocritical action, render him the destroyer of himself.[28]

In summary, traditionalists have established rival altars around the world and will only worship where their personal ideological preferences are met. They will not attend the form of the Mass celebrated by the Pope and the bishops of the world, declaring that it is in fact a sin or harmful to one's faith to do so. If circumstances demand they attend another Latin Mass, they refuse to receive the Eucharist. They assemble apart from, and in opposition to, the local bishop, receiving the Eucharist from the hands of wandering priests and bishops who have not been given jurisdiction to do so. They hold their own conferences, their own pilgrimages, and their own fundraisers, none of which are connected to the diocese or to the rest of the Church. They establish their own chapels, schools, seminaries, and religious houses, and they discourage their followers from exploring any other religious institutions. They establish what is for all intents and purposes a parallel church. If this does not constitute a "refusal of communion," what does?

---

[28] Irenaeus, *Against Heresies* (Book IV, Chapter 18), retrieved from New Advent, https://www.newadvent.org/fathers/0103418.htm

10.

A Self-Enclosed Circle

Traditionalists frequently use Pope Benedict XVI's quote about the *versus populum* ("facing the people") orientation in their criticisms of the Novus Ordo Missae. Benedict XVI took issue with this particular liturgical option, describing it as a "self-enclosed circle"[1] of the priest and community (although he went on to concede that "a face-to-face exchange between proclaimer and hearer does make sense"[2] during the Liturgy of the Word, and that to simply revoke *versus populum* wholesale would be a mistake, as "[n]othing is more harmful to the liturgy than a constant activism, even if it seems to be for the sake of genuine renewal"[3]). The debate over *ad orientem* and *versus populum* orientation continues, and the Church has permitted either one. I do not assume to have an answer to this debate. However, I do think this presents an opportunity for some self-reflection on the part of the traditionalists.

We see strikingly similar language being employed by the former pontiff when, in his book *Dogma and Preaching*, he describes Catholic communities who do not engage in efforts of evangelization and outreach:

---

[1] Ratzinger, *The Spirit of the Liturgy*, 80.

[2] Ibid., 81.

[3] Ibid., 83.

On the one hand, there must be the interior self-fulfillment of the faith, in which it is perpetually received anew and at the same time becomes richer in a history of growth and life. On the other hand, *there must be a constant surpassing of the closed circle and a proclamation of the faith to a new world*, in which it must make itself comprehensible once again, so as to bring in people who are still foreign to it. The two are equally important: a Church that still preached, but only internally, that always presupposed the faith as something given and passed it on and developed it further *only within the circle of those who already believed and were taken for granted*, would necessarily become sterile and lose her relevance; she would deprive herself of the impetus of "all shall hear" and thereby contradict the urgent realism of the Christ-event.[4]

The connection between these two passages is clear. Whatever criticisms of this particular liturgical orientation can be leveled, they apply just as well to the ecclesial community as a whole. A church or parish that is content with its own internal life and does not attempt to bring the light of Christ any further than its own doors is not a living, breathing church. This is precisely the issue that was identified by the Church in the decades leading up to Vatican II—that the efforts of evangelization on the part of the laity were, simply put, lacking.

---

[4] Joseph Ratzinger, *Dogma and Preaching*, trans. Michael J. Miller and Matthew J. O'Connell (San Francisco: Ignatius Press, 2011), 20.

Pope St. Paul VI wrote in *Evangelii nuntiandi*, "Anyone who re-reads in the New Testament the origins of the Church, follows her history step by step and watches her live and act, sees that she is linked to evangelization in her most intimate being."[5] To be part of the Church means to bring the Church out to the world, and this call is all the more urgent when the world is besieged by indifferentism, materialism, and agnosticism. Through Vatican II, the Church has urged the faithful to follow the example of Our Lord himself, who said, "I must preach the good news of the kingdom of God to the other cities also; for I was sent for this purpose" (Lk 4:43).

Evangelization is the primary objective of Vatican II, and by rejecting the Council, traditionalists actually are living proof that its objectives must be implemented. They tout their recent growth as proof that their "model" works, but a more honest scrutiny of their growth shows a consistent pattern, one that is attested to by many who have left their ranks. Their communities are primarily made up of multi-generational traditionalists (many of whom attend to avoid family tensions rather than out of a sense of real spiritual investment) and disgruntled Catholics looking for a more reverent place to worship. Appealing to the defense of "by their fruits you shall know them," as the traditionalists often do, shows itself to be a faulty strategy once we realize that the influx of people looking for reverent worship can be found in many other parishes around the world that similarly emphasize devotion and reverence.

---

[5] Paul VI, *Evangelii nuntiandi* (1975), Vatican Archive, https://www.vatican.va/content/paul-vi/en/apost_exhortations/documents/hf_p-vi_exh_19751208_evangelii-nuntiandi.html

There is a risk in relying on the increasing numbers of people in traditionalist communities as proof that their methods work. These newcomers may appreciate the liturgy and the reverence, as they should, but there also may be an underlying cause which is making them only appreciate the external aspects of it. They may simply be satisfied that they are "getting more out of Mass" than they were at their old parish, but the allure cannot be maintained forever. (Ask any teenager who grew up in traditionalist communities if they are entranced by the liturgy. They are not. They are there because they are obliged to be.)

The case for traditionalism might be more convincing if their communities were the source of many converts, but they are not. They bring in very few converts. This is not only an issue in independent groups; even licit groups that celebrate the older form of the Mass suffer from this shortcoming. I can count on one hand the number of adult baptisms that my wife and I (combined) have witnessed during our twenty-five years of frequenting traditionalist or "traditional Catholic" chapels. The unfortunate reality is that these communities do not "go forth" as Vatican II called the laity to do. They remain isolated and content, but they do not bring the heart of the Gospel out. Gary Campbell, the previously cited former SSPX priest, observed that the SSPX might serve as a microcosm of what the Church might be like if no reforms had ever occurred; "a myopic Church incapable of reaching out to the world and – like the SSPX – expecting the world to come on bended knee."[6]

---

[6] Gary Campbell, "Summorum Pontificum: An Unforced Error," Where Peter Is, December 14, 2021. https://wherepeteris.com/summorum-pontificum-an-unforced-error/

The obstacle to evangelization lies in the fact that traditionalist communities do not engage the culture beyond their own boundaries because they are more concerned with defending their particular ideology than with sharing the Gospel. If they remain at a perpetual theological impasse with their Catholic neighbors, how can they be expected to engage further with those who are not familiar with Christianity at all? They have become too fixated on their own inner life to concern themselves with meaningful outreach. Pope Francis decried this behavior in his apostolic exhortation *Evangelii gaudium* and left little doubt as to which demographic his admonishments were directed toward. He said they have adopted a sense of "spiritual worldliness," displaying "an ostentatious preoccupation for the liturgy, for doctrine and for the Church's prestige, but without any concern that the Gospel have a real impact on God's faithful people and the concrete needs of the present time." This causes them to "ultimately trust only in their own powers and feel superior to others because they observe certain rules or remain intransigently faithful to a particular Catholic style from the past."[7]

This ideological stalemate is one of the side effects of self-preservation, which finds its origin in the victim complex that grips traditionalism. From their perspective, the traditionalists are "just doing what the church has always done," and they cannot understand why they are on the receiving end of any reprimands. They see it as their duty to reject any imposed penalties and, therefore, also to reject the

---

[7]   Francis, *Evangelii Gaudium* (2013), Vatican Archive, https://www.vatican.va/content/francesco/en/apost_exhortations/documents/papa-francesco_esortazione-ap_20131124_evangelii-gaudium.html

authority that issues these penalties. This leads to a dead-end spirituality in which they believe persecution is being leveled at them from either side—both from the world and from the Church which should be protecting them from the world. Their movement therefore becomes static and "sterile," as Pope Benedict XVI described. As Msgr. Ronald Knox similarly wrote, all dissenting groups in the history of the Church were "not content to let the wheat and the tares grow side by side until the harvest. [...] Thus a little group of devout souls isolates itself from the rest of society, to form a nucleus for the New Jerusalem; and in doing so it loses touch with the currents of thought that flow outside, grows partisan in its attitude, sterile of new ideas."[8] Communities that constantly feel the need to defend their position and "hold the line," so to speak, are not going to venture out in the world with what they have. They will protect it and try to preserve it from those who want to "persecute" them and suppress what they hold dear. Archbishop Lefebvre referred to his consecrations in 1988 as "Operation Survival," but survival is not life. This is not the model of a spiritually healthy movement.

Traditionalists also find themselves in the awkward position of having a rather deficient motive for evangelization. What kind of success could one hope for in trying to convince outsiders that the spiritual fulfillment they seek can be found in the Catholic Church, yet it is also necessary to hold in suspicion everything the Church declares and to operate completely independently of the established hierarchy? If a potential catechumen is dissatisfied with the variety of Scriptural interpretations in Protestantism and is searching for

---

[8] Ronald A. Knox, *Enthusiasm: A Chapter in the History of Religion* (New York; Oxford University Press, 1950), 229-230

stability in the authority that Jesus promised His Church, how would the traditionalist position appeal to them? Attractive liturgies can fulfill their desires for a time, but eventually the lack of unity and the infighting will overshadow the external gratifications, ultimately making the traditionalists' efforts of evangelization fruitless.

The imagery of an enclosed circle is not restricted to the traditionalists' outreach, or lack thereof; it also describes their ideological basis. To them, anything dating past 1965 or so is potentially tainted with Modernism and is therefore untrustworthy. Their formation and catechesis are strictly based in "pre-conciliar" texts and theologies. They reject the Catechism of the Catholic Church promulgated in 1992 and will only use the Catechism of the Council of Trent, or the Baltimore Catechism for younger audiences. They will not use any current Catholic authors or faith formation programs, as they are influenced by Vatican II. Any statement by any pope after Pius XII is useless to them unless it furthers their cause. Pope Paul VI quite accurately wrote to Archbishop Lefebvre in 1976, "In effect you and those who are following you are endeavouring to come to a standstill at a given moment in the life of the Church."[9]

If what the traditionalists have is so effective and is the antidote for all the errors and confusion in the Church, what good can come from withdrawing to the peripheries and letting the crisis fester? Do the traditionalists believe that their duty is not to bring the Gospel to the world, but to simply outlast the error and "remain faithful to Tradition" until the Church comes back to them? It certainly seems

---

[9] Pope Paul VI's Letter to Archbishop Marcel Lefebvre, September 11, 1976, as quoted in Likoudis and Whitehead, *The Pope, The Council, and The Mass,* 350

this way; Archbishop Lefebvre said, "[I]n several years—I do not know how many, only the Good Lord knows how many years it will take for Tradition to find its rights in Rome—we will be embraced by the Roman authorities, who will thank us for having maintained the Faith[.]"[10] This again proves that their objective is merely survival, not accepting the mission of the Church.

Yet another passage from Gary Campbell's letter touches on this topic.

> So will I return to the Novus Ordo, as the dog returns to his vomit? No, I shall return to the Catholic Church. I labour under no illusions. I am not going to greener pastures. The Lord's field is brown and harsh. I have no doubt there will be many times I will sigh for the security and peace I enjoyed, but what kind of security? What kind of peace? We have created for ourselves a nice little air-conditioned world, with our churches and solemn liturgies, our sermons. It is peaceful and sunny, but outside, the storm rages. The world of the storm we shut out, condemn. But it is there where God's People are, just as much as they are in our little sphere. And [they are] just as much children of the Creator as we are. As I was saying, the Lord's field is brown and harsh, but still, it is our country, our homeland. It begs for tillers to rejuvenate it. The Society cannot do it. It has shut itself out.[11]

---

[10] Marcel Lefebvre, "1988 Episcopal Consecrations sermon," SSPX website. https://sspx.org/en/1988-episcopal-consecrations-sermon-of-archbishop-lefebvre

[11] Campbell, letter to Bishop Bernard Fellay

In a secularized world which so desperately needs the light of Christ's truth, it is a grave mistake to remain in a self-enclosed environment protecting one's preferred rituals and practices. As Bishop Robert Barron wrote, "The moment you exit any Catholic Church in America, you have entered mission territory."[12] The laity *must* go out to the world; they must "go and make disciples of all nations." Jesus said, "Nor do men light a lamp and put it under a bushel, but on a stand, and it gives light to all in the house. Let your light so shine before men, that they may see your good works and give glory to your Father who is in heaven" (Matt 5:15-16). We are called to bring the light to all, not to keep it for ourselves and wait for others to seek it out.

---

[12] Robert Barron, "New Mission Territory" in *The Word on Fire Vatican II Collection: Declarations and Decrees* (Elk Grove Village; Word on Fire, 2023), 246

PART IV

THE FUTURE

11.

A Multiplicity of Sects

In the opening chapter of his novel *Lord of the World*, Msgr. Robert Hugh Benson described a futuristic setting in which Protestantism has died out, saying, "Men do recognise at last that a supernatural Religion involves an absolute authority, and that Private Judgment in matters of faith is nothing else than the beginning of disintegration."[1]

This is a principle that even the traditionalists can agree on. Private judgment is what we as Catholics criticize most heavily on many occasions. We leverage the fact that there are tens of thousands of Protestant denominations to show why we, as one unified church, are in the right, and how remaining under a single authority figure is crucial for the life of the church.

Yet in practice, the traditionalists seem to have forgotten this. Traditionalism attempts to be self-sustaining, supported by its own decisions and its own opinions, rejecting the binding declarations of the supreme authority and content with its own deductions on whether it maintains true tradition. The Church is built on three pillars: Scripture, tradition, and the Magisterium. When one is taken away, the entire structure crumbles. Just as the Protestants split into thousands of independent groups, each of them thinking their interpretation of Scripture is the right one, the traditionalists split into

---

[1] Robert Hugh Benson, *Lord of the World* (1907; Isle of Man, Baronius Press, 2006), 8-9.

factions over their disagreements on what constitutes true tradition and whether it is being maintained in a certain group.

In his encyclical condemning Modernism, Pope St. Pius X wrote, "[T]radition is represented by religious authority, and this both by right and in fact. By right, for it is in the very nature of authority to protect tradition: and in fact, since authority, raised as it is above the contingencies of life, feels hardly, or not at all, the spurs of progress."[2] In their fight against Modernism, the traditionalists seem to have placed themselves within the boundaries of deserving the same reminders issued to their opponents. Tradition and its meaning are not determined by individuals, but by the authority to which all Catholics are subject.

Private judgment naturally begets division, which only begets further division. When one group breaks away, its followers will naturally develop a "better" understanding than the leadership because if the leadership can legitimately break away, why could its subordinates not do the same? They then abandon their post to form their own *petit eglise*, or "little church." The traditionalist movement has given way to the following splinter groups, most of which began with the SSPX and split away due to ideological or theological differences (and this is not an exhaustive list):

-   The Society of St. Pius V (SSPV), which broke away from the SSPX in 1983

---

[2] Pius X, *Pascendi dominici gregis*.

- The Roman Catholic Institute (RCI), established by former SSPX-turned-SSPV priest Donald Sanborn, who went on to become a sedevacantist bishop
- The "Resistance," led by former SSPX bishop Richard Williamson after he was expelled from the Society (and who has since illicitly consecrated several more bishops)
- The SSPX-MC (Marian Corps), led by former SSPX priest David Hewko
- The Institute of the Mother of Good Counsel (IMBC) formed by four Italian priests who left the SSPX
- The now-defunct Priestly Union of Marcel Lefebvre
- The Servants of the Holy Family, established by former SSPX priest Anthony Ward

Some traditionalist priests have also established independent chapels that are not affiliated with any particular group. These priests often obtain episcopal orders from wandering bishops and attempt to construct a solitary group of their own. Some examples include:

- St. Gertrude the Great Traditional Roman Catholic Church in West Chester, OH, founded by former SSPX priest turned sedevacantist bishop Daniel Dolan
- Our Lady of the Pillar Chapel in Louisville, KY, led by former SSPX priest Gavin Bitzer
- St. Dominic Chapel in Highland, MI, led by former SSPX priest and now sedevacantist bishop Robert Neville

-     Our Lady of Mount Carmel Church, Seminary, and Con-
      vent in Boston, KY, led by former SSPX priest and now
      bishop Joseph Pfeiffer

These groups have copious amounts of literature and website
pages explaining why the parent organization they broke away from
had compromised or was otherwise wrong, and often devote more
time and energy expounding on the "errors" of the Church, Vatican
II, and the Novus Ordo Missae than explaining the joy of the faith
and the beauty of Christ's Church. These groups are not united by
any bonds of charity, joy, or peace. The only thing uniting them is
their mutual disapproval of Vatican II, and their agreement that the
Novus Ordo Missae must be abrogated.

Traditionalism is not only beset by warring factions. When one
assumes ultimate authority to themselves, what is to stop them from
claiming the privileges of the See of Peter? Why not assume the role
of the pope since those who occupy the chair are "usurpers" or "heretics?" If the captain of St. Peter's Barque has abandoned it, why not
take control?

This has indeed occurred, with the traditionalist movement
yielding several antipopes. "Pope Michael," or David Bawden, a former SSPX seminarian, declared himself pope in 1990 after a con-
clave of six people (including his parents) elected him. He passed
away on August 2, 2022, and his successor Rogelio Martinez declared himself as "Pope Michael II." Victor von Pentz, another former SSPX seminarian, took the name Pope Linus II in 1994. Friar
Lucian Pulvermacher, who was associated with the "True Catholic
Church" movement (a certain quote of his is worthy of note: "For

eight months I was with the general Latin Mass traditinalists [sic] until I saw there was no unity"[3]), took the name Pope Pius XIII in 1998. The Palmarian Christian Church believes that, following the Second Vatican Council, "the true Church of Christ ceased to be in Rome on the 6th of August, 1978, and from there was translated to El Palmar de Troya, with the election of Pope Saint Gregory XVII as Vicar of Christ, directly by Our Lord Jesus Christ,"[4] and they are currently led by "Pope Peter III" ("Peter II" succeeded the Palmarian's "Gregory XVIII," who abdicated his papacy and admitted the Palmarian Church was "all a set-up"[5]).

Can this be the future of the Church? An unknown number of splinter groups, each of them convinced that they make up the "faithful remnant?" The traditionalists claim that the "pre-conciliar" or "Tridentine" form of Catholicism is the future, but is that realistic to believe, when we can see what a shattered result comes from separating from the Church in spirit and in governance? Can the One, Holy, Catholic, and Apostolic Church be found in a congregation of perhaps several hundred, with a handful of priests and a single bishop, all of whom defy the lawful authorities? Can Our Lord's prayer "that they may be one" (Jn 17:11) be realized in a foray of ideological battles and disunity? As Cardinal Camillo Mazella wrote, "[I]f without the consent of that authority [constituted by Christ],

---

[3] Fr. Lucian Pulvermacher, April 2, 1998, *Warning of "Pope Pius XIII."* https://www.kirchenlehre.com/ truecat.htm

[4] "One, Holy, Catholic, Apostolic, and Palmarian Church," palmarianchurch.org. https://www.palmarianchurch.org/

[5] Javier Martin-Arroyo, "The Palmarian Catholic Church: a lie that lasted 40 years," El Pais, May 26, 2016. https://english.elpais.com/elpais/2016/05/25/inenglish/1464158613_ 478208.html

anyone could establish a just cause for separation by his own judgment, then the government of the Church would be absolutely destroyed. For what authority is that, which the subjects can licitly reject by their own judgment?"[6]

Session III of the First Vatican Council stated, "Everybody knows that those heresies, condemned by the fathers of Trent, which…allowed religious questions to be a matter for the judgment of each individual, have gradually collapsed into a multiplicity of sects, either at variance or in agreement with one another; and by this means a good many people have had all faith in Christ destroyed."[7] This obviously refers to Protestantism, but the applicability here is all too clear. Traditionalism is indeed a "multiplicity of sects" that cannot agree on "religious questions," and which tragically have indeed caused many of the faithful to have "all faith in Christ destroyed." Many simply leave the practice of the faith due to the infighting and confusion of the various traditionalist groups, having decided that if this was the pinnacle of Catholicism, as it claimed to be, it was not worth devoting one's life to.

Ex-SSPX priest Gary Campbell wrote the following in 1999:

We say we cannot follow the Holy Father, except when he confirms tradition. How do we know then, when he confirms the tradition? We know, we affirm, when the present

---

[6] Camillo Mazzella, *De Religione et Ecclesia*, 2nd ed, trans. Eric Hoyle (Rome: Polyglot, 1880) 513-514.

[7] Decrees of the First Vatican Council, Session 3: 24 April 1870, *Dogmatic Constitution on the Catholic Faith*, §5, Papal Encyclicals Online, https://www.papalencyclicals.net/councils/ecum20.htm

Pontiff's statements correspond with those of previous Pontiffs. That judgement is necessarily subjective, and fraught with danger. The private interpretation of acts of the Magisterium is no less uncatholic than the private interpretation of Scripture! How do we know our interpretation is the correct one? And how do we know when a legitimate development of discipline, liturgy or even of doctrine has in fact occurred? Do we all have a grasp of the historical, social, prudential and theological factors that may very well justify such a change? The Holy See has the divine guarantee of the assistance of the Holy Spirit: we, however, do not.[8]

He is not the only former SSPX prelate to recognize the connections. Abbé Emmanuel Berger commented on this as well:

The Protestants, the Jehovah's Witnesses, the Mormons and others all make the Bible say conflicting things. It is easy to demonstrate to them that, as a consequence, Sacred Scripture is not sufficient by itself and that it calls for a Magisterium, an authentic interpreter. Does not the same have to be said for revealed Tradition? Sola Traditio? Everyone lays claim to it to condemn the other. So it is not sufficient by itself; it demands a Magisterium, an authentic interpreter. And this Magisterium is not ourselves, but the Pope. In short, although I hardly remember these words of John Paul II in the Motu Proprio of July 2, 88, Fr. Celier was right to

---

[8] Campbell, letter to Bishop Bernard Fellay.

remind us of them, and I totally agree with them: "At the root of this schismatic act lies an incomplete and contradictory notion of Tradition" (p. 30) "...a false concept of Tradition" (p. 85)[9]

Maintaining tradition by submitting to authority is imperative for the life of the Church. As Pope Benedict XVI wrote:

> Only the unity of the Church's faith and her authority, which is binding on each member, assures us that we are not following human opinions and adhering to self-made party groupings but that we belong to the Lord and are obeying him. There is a great danger today that the Church will disintegrate into religious parties that rally around individual teachers or preachers. And if this is so, what was true then is true once more: I am Apollo's, I am Paul's, I am Cephas', and we end by making even Christ into a party.[10]

The results of the former pontiff's warning are clearly manifested in the traditionalist movement. Having the best of intentions to worship reverently and find reliable catechesis, the faithful have fallen into the snares of adhering to the opinions of individual priests or bishops. Are they not saying, "I belong to Lefebvre; I belong to Williamson; I belong to Pivarunas?" Do prelates guarantee salvation in their dissent against divinely instituted authority?

---

[9] Berger, letter to Bishop Bernard Fellay.

[10] Ratzinger, *Called to Communion*, 163-164.

Pope Francis referred to the same passage from St. Paul in his letter accompanying *Traditionis custodes,* in which he explained his reasons for restricting the use of the 1962 missal:

[E]ver more plain in the words and attitudes of many is the close connection between the choice of celebrations according to the liturgical books prior to Vatican Council II and the rejection of the Church and her institutions in the name of what is called the "true Church." One is dealing here with comportment that contradicts communion and nurtures the divisive tendency —"I belong to Paul; I belong instead to Apollo; I belong to Cephas; I belong to Christ" —against which the Apostle Paul so vigorously reacted.[11]

Traditionalists will balk at the accusation that they claim to preserve the "true church," but Pope Francis' statement is not inaccurate. The traditionalists have created a catalog of verbiage for their position, including such terms as "the Novus Ordo church," the "conciliar church," or the "Modernist church." They clearly see themselves as a distinct entity and only claim to be in union with the Church when their position is challenged and shown to be inconsistent with the true understanding of communion. (One has to wonder why they so vehemently insist on being in union with the

---

[11] Francis, "Letter of the Holy Father Francis to the bishops of the whole world, that accompanies the Apostolic Letter motu proprio data Traditionis custodes," July 16, 2021, Vatican Archive, https://www.vatican.va/content/francesco/en/letters/2021/documents/20210716-lettera-vescovi-liturgia.html

Church when they also claim the Church is riddled with error, overcome by Modernism, and even in a state of apostasy.) Archbishop Lefebvre himself said in the sermon before the 1988 consecrations that the seminarians he illicitly ordained had approached him to "receive a true ordination to the priesthood, to say the true Sacrifice of Calvary, the true Sacrifice of the Mass, and to give you the true Sacraments, true doctrine, the true catechism."[12] Does this leave any doubt as to whether they see the Church of Christ as separate and "untrue?"

If traditionalists cannot agree on disciplinary issues, how can they be expected to agree on doctrinal issues, which are ultimately the deciding factor in their reconciliation with the Church? Disagreements are the hallmark of the various traditionalist factions, from whether the new rite of ordination is valid to whether the leadership of a group has compromised their values by engaging in discussions with Rome (both of which have served as the deciding factor of different splinter groups). The "ravening wolves" Our Lord warned us of have noticed the discord and are circling the fences, but if the shepherds are too occupied finding fault with their fellow shepherds to notice, will they be prepared to address the real threats to the Church?

We cannot expect the future to be in the hands of opposing factions, all of which have decided to separate themselves from Holy Mother Church in unity and governance. In decrying the strife between prelates outside their own spheres, traditionalists also must

---

[12] Marcel Lefebvre, "1988 Episcopal Consecrations sermon," SSPX website. https://sspx.org/en/1988-episcopal-consecrations-sermon-of-archbishop-lefebvre

have the honesty to acknowledge the plank in their own eye and be willing to submit to one singular authority. In the words of Pope Pius XI, "How so great a variety of opinions can make the way clear to effect the unity of the Church We know not; that unity can only arise from one teaching authority, one law of belief and one faith of Christians."[13]

---

[13] Pius XI, *Mortalium Animos* (1928), Vatican Archive, https://www.vatican.va/content/pius-xi/en/encyclicals/documents/hf_p-xi_enc_19280106_mortalium-animos.html

12.

When Will the Crisis End?

Traditionalism relies upon a position that is intellectually irresponsible at best, and theologically absurd at worst; namely, it makes the very concrete assertion that an unprecedented crisis justifies an unprecedented response, while at the same time avoiding any concrete assertion as to *when* the crisis will end and *how* the response will cease. It is therefore incumbent on the traditionalists to answer one very simple question. When will the crisis end?

This question, in my estimation, is the decisive factor on which traditionalism rests. If there is no answer, the entire movement lacks any foundation. But there must be an answer, if they want to justify such an irregular ministry. They admit that their pastoral activities at least *appear* to contradict many previous disciplines upheld by the Church and that their only purpose is to respond to a perceived crisis which apparently did not exist 60 years ago (or at least not to the extent that it necessitated such a ministry). The crisis must end at some point. But to provide an answer, one must also know who decides this, and how they arrived at the decision they did. Can that information be determined?

I have posed this question to many people and have never received a satisfactory answer. Most evade the question entirely. Some scoff and say that it is a ridiculous question. Some shrug and say we cannot know. Some simply repeat that we are in fact in a crisis, and the traditionalists are just doing what must be done. Very few attempt to pinpoint something objective, but when they do, their answer falls short after examining it. Let us consider the typical responses to see if it is possible to provide an answer to this question.

The most common answer is that the Novus Ordo Missae is to blame. Is the crisis over once the 1962 missal is reinstated as the norm and the missal of Pope St. Paul VI is abrogated? Obviously, the answer is no. Traditionalists discourage or even forbid their followers from attending the Latin Mass celebrated elsewhere, on the basis that the priests or communities offering them "accept Vatican II" and are therefore "compromised."[1] They discourage attending diocesan Latin Masses for fear of the priest being "tainted with Modernism," which he may impart on the faithful during his homily. Even if every priest in the world celebrated Mass according to this missal, it would not change their outlook. Clearly the issue runs deeper.

Is the crisis over when Vatican II is removed from the history books, and the Church admits that the largest gathering of bishops in her history was simply a mistake? Once again, the answer is most emphatically in the negative. The world would still be entrenched in materialism and atheism that would continue to dominate society, and the defection from all forms of religion would continue.

Is the crisis over when the rites of the sacraments are reverted to the old forms, and all priests ordained under the new rite die out, removing any doubt about the sacraments' efficacy or whatever

---

[1] Former traditionalists have commented on this inconsistency, recounting how they were urged to pray for the intention that Pope Benedict XVI would allow wider use of the 1962 missal, but then when he did so in 2007, they were still forbidden to attend these masses.

other issue the traditionalists find with them? Again, the answer is no. Literature, theology, church architecture, and all else would still reflect the development of the Church since the Council. Again, if priests today who offer sacraments according to the old form, like the FSSP, should be avoided because they "accept Vatican II," how would the situation change if every priest in the world offered them?

Traditionalists still invoke this state of necessity when FSSP or ICKSP parishes are nearby, leading to the conclusion that it is not only a matter of having sacraments and Mass under a certain form; the priests offering them apparently must be free of a certain ideology as well. This is confusing; is an FSSP priest somehow unable to consecrate the Eucharist, or witness a marriage? Does a priest's internal disposition or acceptance of a certain proposition (the teachings of a council, for instance) rob him of the ability to offer sacraments validly and licitly? It is not the responsibility of the laity to know their parish priest's personal opinions. These have no effect on the sacraments being offered. And what sort of Church would it be if priests could discourage the reception of sacraments from a brother priest because of his personal opinion on a given topic?

Is the crisis over when the members of the hierarchy renounce their alleged Modernism and "return to tradition?" How would that happen? A simple declaration or signature is obviously not sufficient; they would need to act on it. And again, this needs some objectively verifiable criterion. Does it mean censoring or defrocking those who are "modernists"? How do we know who they are? Does it mean redacting problematic books or theology manuals? How do we know which ones those are? Who decides these things? It again becomes a matter of a group's placing their own judgements and authority over those of the Church. Deposing the modernists would also go hand in hand with erasing the Council. Obviously, it is not enough to state or sign a renouncement; one would have to put it into force somehow, and renouncing Modernism would mean nothing if the Council and its reforms were allowed to remain.

Surely there must be a concrete, identifiable action that can be taken to dispel the crisis. One suspects that, for the traditionalists, nothing less than a complete reversal of the last sixty years will suffice. But even if this were somehow possible, the world and the Church would still be plagued by the societal and cultural issues described in previous chapters, presumably meaning the crisis would continue until…when?

The traditionalists cannot provide answers to these questions because quite frankly, there are no answers. Any response would be entirely subjective and therefore unsustainable. But there *must* be some objective criteria; otherwise, if one cannot definitively say when and how this crisis will end, one cannot say when or how it began, and it devolves into a nebulous, generic concept that anyone can invoke if they need an all-encompassing justification for what would normally be an illicit ministry.

And when all is said and done, none of the above propositions even matter at all, because then the second question is: who determines this? The traditionalists? The Church is not the one determining it, so that places each traditionalist group as its own authority in this scenario.

Allow me to present a series of questions that further illustrate the subjectivity of this crisis. What happens if there is a dispute amongst the leadership of a particular group as to when the crisis is over? Take the SSPX as an example, which currently has three bishops. What if, in Bishop Fellay's opinion, the crisis has been resolved, but in Bishop de Galarreta's opinion, it has not? Can he then continue to operate with whatever priests side with him? Or does Bishop Fellay's opinion hold more weight, making the matter final? None of the three bishops hold any more authority than the other, so if there were a disagreement, there does not seem to be a legitimate way to resolve it. And so, if one decided he did not want to relinquish his supposed authority, he need only claim there is still a state of necessity. Denying this would only introduce further confusion, as they would need to provide some quantifiable metric as to why one was right and the other was wrong, bringing the issue full circle and demanding that there be some objectively verifiable criterion.

Even supposing the traditionalists did lay out a specific set of criteria to be met, what is to say they could not simply change their mind? How would their own declarations bind them? They would be submitting to their own subjective conclusions, not to any authoritative judgment from a superior, and so it would hold no actual weight. If their terms were to be met, all they need to do to retain their ministry is say that the first decision was not good enough and lay out a new set of criteria. Is the crisis over? Not if they are the ones deciding the terms. Why is the first set of criteria any more authoritative than the second?

Yet another consideration: why would one traditionalist group be able to determine when the crisis is over, but not another? If we do not know when, how, and why the crisis is over, and there is no answer for who has the final say in this matter, why would the decision of one group bind another? For example, if the SSPX decides the crisis is over, but the CMRI disagrees, may the CMRI continue to operate? If not, why not? Does the SSPX exercise authority over them? And if so, why? Is their word more authoritative than the SSPX's? Again, one bishop does not hold any more authority than another, so neither option works, and one could appeal to this defense to continue their ministry while another thinks it has passed. It is certainly an odd sort of crisis which affects some clergy and not others.

It is the same convoluted situation that the sedevacantists face. If there is no pope, when and how does a legitimate pope take office, and who determines how that happens? And if a solution is presented, from whom did that specific group or person who presented it receive the authority to do so? What makes their opinion any more binding than another's? Is the power of the See of Peter subject to the determinations of a lay person? And if one sedevacantist group concedes that this new pope is indeed the pope, does that bind all other sedevacantist groups? Can they continue in their belief that the seat is still vacant? Whose judgment is correct?[2]

It should be clear after this series of questions that this crisis is necessarily subjective. There is no answer for when it has been dispelled. The traditionalists will continue to minister, splintering into

---

[2] A common belief in sedevacantist circles is that the next "true" pope will be appointed by some form of unmistakable divine intervention or miraculous event. One finds a great irony here, in that they recognize miraculous evidence as proof of God's will, yet do not hold their ministry and ecclesiastical "mission" to the same standard.

smaller and smaller groups, each of them thinking they have the true faith and each of them continuing to denounce the other. But there will come a time when they will need to admit that the crisis is over. Even they must acknowledge that the Church does not and cannot exist in a perpetual and indefinite crisis. It must end at some point. So, when does it? Who decides this? How? When it does, they would essentially have to voluntarily surrender their entire ministry. As Pope St. Paul VI stipulated to Archbishop Lefebvre in 1976, reconciliation with the Church would require that the SSPX's chapels, seminaries, and other institutions be handed over to Rome, and their future usage (or closure) would be dependent on the local bishop's decision in whichever diocese they were established. Even if they were granted the status of a personal prelature, like Opus Dei (although this has been proposed and rejected before), they would be subject to the Church in a capacity which they have thus far refused. Is this something they are prepared to do?

The crisis is far too broad to be resolved by the conflicting opinions of various autonomous communities. During the time of the Arian heresy in the early centuries of the Church, St. Jerome wrote, "The world groaned to find itself Arian." As widespread as this heresy may have been, it was only throughout the known world at the time. In today's day and age, when technology connects one corner of the globe to another, communication is instantaneous, and the world cares for nothing beyond that which it can comprehend, it might be said that the world cheered to find itself atheist. It was content within its own horizons and dismissed as superstition anything beyond that. The crisis began when the world collectively rejected God and put itself in His place; it will only be dispelled when secularism and materialism are supplanted by surrender to the divine, and when the Gospel is lived out as a culture and as a people.

As Christopher Dawson wrote, "The only real solution is to change the cultural environment which has made it possible for this unnatural state of things to develop." He continues:

> The present situation is that modern secularized culture has become a closed world and has lost all contact with the higher world of spiritual reality. In the past this higher world was rendered intelligible and visible to Western man through the medium of Christian culture, which provided a whole series of ways of approach adapted to the different types of mind and the different forms of intellectual activity. Today all these avenues have become closed by ignorance, prejudice or neglect, and they have to be re-opened by the spiritual and intellectual action of Catholics, each working in his own field towards the common end[.] [...] What is vital is to recover the moral and spiritual foundations on which the lives of both the individual and the culture depend: to bring home to the average man that religion is not a pious fiction which has nothing to do with the facts of life, but that it is concerned with realities, that it is in fact the pathway to reality and the law of life. [...] *And so it is not enough for Catholics to maintain a high standard of religious practice within the Catholic community, it is also necessary for them to build a bridge of understanding out into secular culture and to act*

as interpreters of the Christian faith to the world outside the Church.[3]

Dawson's observations could almost be said to be prophetic. His timing is indeed impeccable; just one year after he wrote these words, Pope John XXIII opened the Second Vatican Council, citing the same urgent necessity for a renewal of Christian life in a post-Christian culture, and urging all Catholics to not only know and live their faith fully, but imbue their environments with it, so that it is not a worship-only faith, but a lived faith. As Pope Pius XI wrote in the 1930s, and which is all the more applicable today, "As in all the stormy periods of the history of the Church, the fundamental remedy today lies in a sincere renewal of private and public life according to the principles of the Gospel by all those who belong to the Fold of Christ, that they may be in truth the salt of the earth to preserve human society from total corruption."[4] The solution is, simply put, a restoration of all things in Christ, by showing the world through our actions and our example that He is the Way, the Truth, and the Life. How exactly we can hope to accomplish this, and why moving forward with the Church is the only option, will be explored in the next and final chapter.

---

[3] Dawson, 175-176.

[4] Pius XI, *Divini redemptoris.*

13.

The New Springtime

Understanding the state of the world and the Church as they existed for several hundred years before Vatican II, and understanding that the Council's objective was to rejuvenate the evangelizing energies of the laity, it should come as no surprise that it called for a reform of such magnitude. In his homily for Pentecost Sunday in 1998, Pope St. John Paul II referred to this renewal as a "new springtime"[1] that had been brought about by the Holy Spirit after Vatican II. This description continues to be cited in the aftermath of the Council, both by those who patiently wait for its reforms to bear fruit in the wake of a flawed implementation, and by the traditionalists who see no indications of a springtime on the horizon.

We will first examine the position of the latter group. The traditionalists believe that widespread liturgical abuse, decrease in numbers of those who regularly attend Mass, poor catechetical formation, and other tragedies are proof that Vatican II's reforms were a failure, signaling a bitter winter instead of a blossoming spring. To them, the Council is still only being pursued by a demographic of progressive prelates who were alive when it occurred, and the winter that the Church currently finds herself in will dissipate once these

---

[1] Homily of His Holiness John Paul II, Sunday, 31 May 1998, Vatican Archive, https://www.vatican.va/content/john-paul-ii/en/homilies/1998/documents/hf_jp-ii_hom_31051998.html

prelates are no longer attempting to foist the Council's flawed program onto the laity. Traditionalists see it as their duty to resist these reforms until the Council dwindles into obscurity and "traditional Catholicism" wins the day.

This position displays an approach toward the Church that is rooted in the same error as the crisis—namely, reliance on functionality. Traditionalists are quick to argue that the reformed liturgy, the new catechism, and the Church's new approach to the world did not produce the renewal of faith that they promised. But at the same time, traditionalists fail to realize that perhaps true faith was lacking in the hearts of the laity, and that a renewal of faith as envisioned by the Council is not something that can happen within a few years or even decades. It cannot be said that a certain missal or catechism does not "work," as if they functioned like a piece of machinery that operated more efficiently than another. We should not dismiss them as failures so quickly when the scope of the reform is much broader than anything that can be measured in such short terms.

In examining the root of the crisis as I have done in the opening chapter, one can also deduce that the traditionalists unfortunately only perpetuate this crisis, and it is impossible for their ministry to serve as the solution to it. I do not intend to imply they are promoting agnosticism or surrendering to "the world," but their *modus operandi* is clearly a manifestation of this crisis of authority.

Consider the following facts. Traditionalists disregard the necessary spiritual realities underlying the sacraments and the authority of the Church for the sake of their functionality. As long as they have valid bishops who can consecrate valid priests, and have valid priests who can administer valid sacraments, it does not matter that they do not operate in communion with the Church or with the lawful authorities, or even with other traditionalist groups.[2] For them, the Eucharist is no longer the Eucharist of the whole Church; it is that of a select few who agree with each other on certain topics. Bishops are no longer truly bishops; they are priest makers, confirmands, church consecrators, nothing more than living tools to ensure an apostolate does not die out. Priests are ordained simply for the sake of providing sacraments in a "time of need," and as substitutes for the lawful pastors of a diocese, no less.[3] Catholic communities are no longer about living and growing in union with other communities; they exist to offer an alternative to the community down the street. The Church is no longer even the Church; it is reduced to a circle of believers who profess to maintain "true Tradition" while they claim

---

[2] One must not make the mistake of thinking that it is legitimate to receive or participate in certain sacraments as long as they meet the minimum criteria of being valid. Liceity, or legality, of the sacraments is no less important. With regard to sacraments being administered when a priest has no jurisdiction to do so, the answer to question 1004 of the Baltimore Catechism quoted in Chapter 4 goes on to say, "Any use of sacred power without authority is sinful, and all who take part in such ceremonies are guilty of sin."

[3] It should come as no surprise that traditionalist priests experience burnout at extremely high rates. For all their claims about explosive growth, estimates put the total number of ordained SSPX priests around 1400, yet they have only about 700 serving today. In a personal correspondence with the author, a former SSPX priest referred to the demands of their ministry as "dehumanizing" and "a form of abuse," and said he had heard brother priests express the same sentiment. Their ranks continue to diminish due to priests reconciling with Rome, departing for independent ministries, being laicized at their request, or following the slope to sedevacantism.

that rest of the One, Holy, Catholic, and Apostolic Church flounders in error and remains stuck in a rut of confusion and heresy.

This is the antithesis of Catholic life. It has been subordinated to the functions of its various parts, attempting to construct a whole that can still stand on its own, but that does not have a universal cohesion. Faith is put in certain expressions and rites and prayers, but these things are divorced from the Church as a body. Professing faith and hope in God while worshiping independently of those to whom He has entrusted the guidance of His Church is putting one's faith in a God who is disconnected from His Church—a "past" God or an idealized God. In reducing the faith to mere functionality, and by doing this in a state of unabashed disobedience to lawful spiritual authority, the traditionalists are only adding fuel to the flames of the crisis.

The solution is not embedded in a specific liturgical book or in certain practices that once dominated the field of Catholic piety. But we also cannot make the mistake of thinking that a new mode of worship or a new catechism with less archaic language can generate this renewal on their own. Pope Francis said that "it is not enough to reform the liturgical books; the mentality of the people must be reformed as well."[4]

In the Church's history, councils have taken about one hundred years to be fully realized and implemented. There are a number of positive reforms that indicate a true renewal is on the horizon, showing that the buds of this springtime have indeed started to blossom

---

[4] Elise Harris, "For Pope Francis, 'the liturgical reform is irreversible'," Catholic News Agency, August 24, 2017. https://insidethevatican.com/news/pope-francis-liturgical-reform-irreversible/

halfway through the century. Perhaps the most significant reform is the Church's deliberate decision to move away from the spirit of anathematizing and restricting, and to instead resort to exhortations and positive growth.[5] For centuries, the Church had been maintaining a defensive stance, reinforcing her ramparts with prohibitions and denunciations. Now, in a time that had been overcome by what Pope Benedict XVI would later term the "dictatorship of relativism,"[6] the Church deemed it necessary to abandon this defensive stance and pivot to an "offensive" one. As Joseph Ratzinger wrote, "[T]he old policy of exclusiveness, condemnation, and defense leading to an almost neurotic denial of all that was new" was to be discontinued, and the Church intended to "turn over a new leaf and move on into a new and positive encounter with its own origins[.]"[7]

Practically speaking, it would have been futile to continue with an approach that fewer and fewer people would submit to, but the Church in her wisdom knew that it was not only a matter of practicality. It was a matter of fulfilling mankind's deepest desires, which it was attempting to find in the morass of secular culture and all its

---

[5] The traditionalists should in fact be grateful for Vatican II and its insistence on moving on from the position of opposing and anathematizing. If the Church had not done this, she surely would have condemned their actions with such strong terms as she had done in the past, considering the multitude of canons, decrees, and other declarations listed in preceding chapters which they blatantly violate.

[6] Homily of his Eminence Card. Joseph Ratzinger, Dean of the College of Cardinals, April 18, 2005, Vatican Archive, https://www.vatican.va/gpII/documents/homily-pro-eligendo-pontifice_20050418_en.html

[7] Ratzinger, *Theological Highlights of Vatican II*, 44.

temptations. Retreating to a vantage point and condemning from a distance would not prompt anyone to search for happiness through the Church, but the positive care referred to by Joseph Ratzinger would make known the fact that the Church offers something not found anywhere else. It truly would show that the Church was a mother, welcoming those who sought refuge.

Another positive reform is a restoration of the Scriptures and the Church Fathers in the field of moral theology. One sees this perhaps most explicitly in the Catechism of the Catholic Church, published in 1992, which has countless citations from both sources, and moderates the old approach of moral obligations. It first expounds on the faith through the articles of the Creed, then the sacramental economy, and only when these are thoroughly explained does it venture into the moral life, presenting it as "life in Christ." As Fr. Pinckaers explains, "[T]he *Catechism* situates the moral life in the context of the human person's natural desire for happiness, for which the divine promises and the Evangelical Beatitudes are a response."[8] This Catechism requires thorough study; it is not a series of questions and answers that can be memorized (which have their place but are better as an introduction than a complete form of catechesis).

The emphasis on the biblical roots of Catholicism has also become much more prominent in recent decades, focusing especially on the significance of the covenants and our personal relationship with Christ, and presenting the opportunity for Catholics to anchor their faith in the Gospel more than in external rituals. This has

---

[8] Pinckaers, *Morality*, 59.

strengthened ecumenism and provided common ground for dialogue with Protestants, who (it must be admitted) have historically been much more biblically literate than Catholics. New apostolates like the Augustine Institute and the St. Paul Center for Biblical Theology, catechetical material from organizations like Ascension and Word on Fire, apologetics organizations like Catholic Answers, and opportunities for young Catholics such as FOCUS (Fellowship of Catholic University Students) all show that Vatican II is indeed bearing fruit. The laity have heard the call to evangelize and have taken up the challenge. Not to mention, it is undeniable that the liturgical abuse which was common in the decades after the Council has greatly dissipated, and church remodels that restore traditional art and architecture are becoming more and more common.

These are seeds that have been planted with the expectation of an abundant harvest in the Church, but they will take time. Emerging from a spiritual outlook that had been dominant for four hundred years is not something that will happen within a generation or two. These are far-reaching changes that must trickle into the culture, starting with the family and moving up to the parish, the diocese, and eventually the level of the country and the nation. As Fr. Pinckaers wrote, "The involvement of the Holy Spirit in our growth in virtue shows us that the Spirit acts in us through the normal paths of daily effort...He moves like sap, whose movement we neither see nor sense...Yet his gradual push, alone with our confident fidelity, prepares the way for the flowering of spring and the growth of autumn."[9]

---

[9] Ibid., 88.

The weeds will inevitably grow alongside the wheat; we have seen this in too many unfortunate cases already. But that does not justify cutting down the remaining wheat and pretending as though the field had never been sown. Patience, obedience, and trust in the Lord to guide His Church is the answer. "For as the heavens are higher than the earth, so are my ways higher than your ways and my thoughts than your thoughts" (Is 55:9).

Made in the USA
Columbia, SC
04 July 2024

30a1db8d-9caa-4e23-a6d6-628b330521e4R01